THE BISHOPS WALTHAM BRANCH

ROGER SIMMONDS & KEVIN ROBERTSON

WILD SWAN PUBLICATIONS LTD.

FOR HARRY NEWMAN

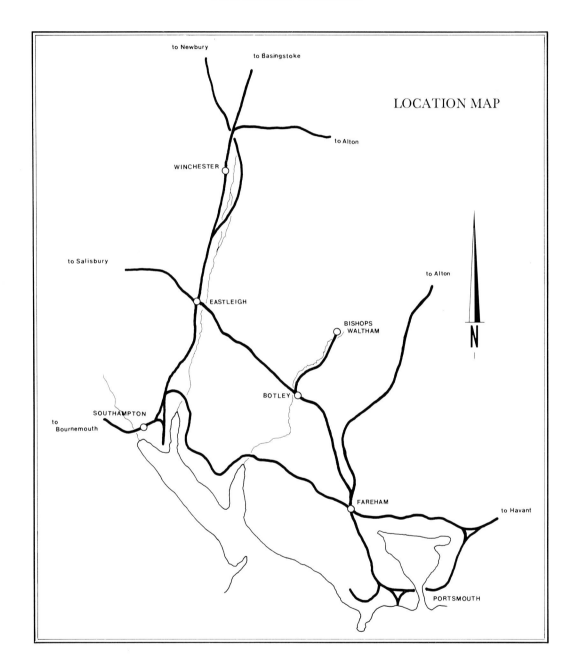

LOCATION MAP

Designed by Paul Karau
Printed by Amadeus Press, Huddersfield

Published by
WILD SWAN PUBLICATIONS LTD.
1-3 Hagbourne Road, Didcot, Oxon. OX11 8DP

CONTENTS

INTRODUCTION

Throughout its existence of just under a century, the Bishops Waltham branch was always very much a local affair. The line was, and indeed still is, held in enormous affection by people in this delightful part of Hampshire. An early casualty of enterprising bus companies, passenger services were curtailed at the end of 1932. Fortunately, road services were not ready to handle all the nation's freight so goods traffic continued over the line for three further decades, enough to enable another generation to discover the delights of this short but attractive line with that wondrous and unique station building at its terminus.

It was that feature that kindled my interest in the branch in the early 1960s when passing through Bishops Waltham. Although sadly deteriorated by this time and minus platform canopy, it remained as significant a landmark in the town as the Abbey ruins. It was indeed a monstrous act that May day in 1965 when the bulldozers moved in to demolish it.

The locals of Botley, Curdridge, Durley and Bishops Waltham still talk fondly of their line, and hold memories which have transcended the fifty-five years or so since the last passenger working of the 'Waltham Jack' — a time when the railway was an integral part of the way of life in the communities it served, before Philistines destroyed so much of our railway network in the name of progress.

The line was born out of the tenacity of Sir Arthur Helps with the prospect of further extension ultimately to provide a through route, alas cruelly curtailed by the financial instability of the little company. The years of bankruptcy were mercifully extinguished by the LSWR and led to a period of modest prosperity, the branch enjoying its heyday in the years surrounding the First War.

Picture, then, the scene at Botley at this time. A mother with two young children hurrying over the footbridge to catch the Bishops Waltham steam railmotor waiting in the bay. Guard George Padwick stroking his moustache and glancing at his watch, notices the approaching entourage and courteously opens a compartment door and helps the party aboard. Briefly exchanging a few words, he raises a hand to Driver Perkins who by now had extinguished the remains of a cigarette and ensconced himself in the small cab of the railmotor. The single coach pulls away from the platform, acceleration increasing as the single line tablet is safely collected from the signalman and the train curves away from the main line for the gentle 4½-mile trip to 'Waltham.

Roger Simmonds

BISHOPS WALTHAM RAILWAY COMPANY.

Capital £16,000, in Shares of £10 each.

Nº 442

£10 SHARE.

This is to Certify that *John Alldin Moore* of Cannon Street West City Merchant is the Proprietor of the £10 Share Number 442 in the above Company, subject to the Rules and Regulations of the said Company.

Given under the Common Seal of the said Company the First day of August 1862

Rook Franklin, Secretary.

CHAPTER ONE
'EARLY SCHEMES'
1860 to 1863

THE small Hampshire town of Bishops Waltham lies at the head of the Hamble River some nine miles from the estuary at Southampton Water, and dates from Roman times where a settlement existed near the old Roman road from Portchester to Winchester. The name 'Waltham', meaning 'the settlement in a wood', derives from mediaeval times when it was called South Waltham to distinguish it from another Waltham in the north of the county. However, when the stately palace of Bishop Henry of Blois was built in 1138, the prefix 'South' was soon exchanged for 'Bishops'.

As the town developed, a considerable trade took place in tanning and malting, and later the market and fair were important features in what was largely an agricultural and fruit growing area. By the middle of the 19th century, despite the existence of some 'light industry' which included brewing and several flour mills, unemployment in the surrounding area was very high, not helped by the national financial depression and poor state of the money market at the time. A local gentleman, Mr. Helps (later Sir Arthur Helps), was mindful of this situation and purchased land to the north-west of the town on which clay beds were located, and formed the Bishops Waltham Clay Company, providing much needed employment. The geology of the area was described in an 1875 directory: 'the soil is partly clay with other parts sand and loam, the subsoil is gravel, chalk and flint'.

Sir Arthur Helps was to prove a great benefactor to Bishops Waltham, being instrumental in the establishment of both the Gas Works and Water Works around the same period (1862–3), the former being one of several small works being established in the County at this time.

FIRST PROPOSALS
With such rapid development taking place, the need for rail access to the town was paramount. The first serious proposals which would have caused a railway to pass through the town appeared in the 1861 Parliamentary Sessions. The Petersfield and Botley Railway was to commence at a junction with the London & South Western Railway at Petersfield by way of East Meon, Meonstoke and Bishops Waltham, to connect with an east/west junction at Botley on the L & SWR Bishopstoke (Eastleigh) to Gosport line of 1841. A second Bill, the Petersfield, Bishops Waltham and Botley Railway, also appeared in the same session although it also encompassed proposed extensions to Netley Hospital and Southampton.

This latter proposal stemmed from the promoters of the Petersfield Railway who, having been granted an Act of the 23rd July 1860 for their line from Midhurst to Petersfield, were ambitious for further expansion. They had found a sympathetic ear from the inhabitants of Southampton whose encouragement was clear from a resolution approved by the town's Chamber of Commerce in August 1860:

'That at the present time great inconvenience arises from the want of more direct communication by railway with the south-eastern counties of England. That a line from Southampton to Petersfield in connection with the Midhurst and Mid-Sussex Railway, would afford the accommodation required, not only by the inhabitants of Southampton but also by those of Bishops Waltham, Droxford and other parts of the locality, at present, wholly deficient of railway accommodation.'

At a cost of about £260,000 the $23\frac{1}{2}$ mile line would have diverged from the PR line as authorised, and passed by way of East Meon, Meonstoke, Droxford and Bishops Waltham, crossing the LSWR Gosport line and the Bishopstoke–Southampton main line near South Stoneham. A terminus was to be made in Southampton on the west side of the town.

Rejection of the Bill by the Commons Committee in 1861 came as quite a shock to the PR Company and it soon became obvious that the LSW, who had objected to the Bill, were vehemently opposed to any schemes 'unjustly invasive' upon its existing territory. The threat of a second attempt by the PR for a Bill in the 1862 Sessions was enough for the LSW to offer to purchase the Petersfield Railway Company outright for £110,000. The PR directors accepted and with the sale the Southampton extension disappeared.

The failure of the 1861 schemes caused much disappointment in Bishops Waltham and some determined inhabitants led by Helps hurriedly prepared Bills for the 1862 Sessions. These were entitled the 'Bishops Waltham, Botley and Bursledon Railway' and consisted of three separate lines. Railway No. 1 (3m. 41ch.) was to commence in a field to the north of Bishops Waltham and the Fishers Pond turnpike road and terminate in the same parish by a junction with the L & SWR about ten chains to the north-west of Botley station. Railway No. 2 (3m. 18ch.) was to continue from this point, crossing the L & SWR and terminate in the parish of Bursledon. Railway No. 3 (0m. 31ch.) was a short spur commencing by a junction with the L & SWR on the south side of their line and terminating in a junction with Railway No. 2. Authorisation was sought to form a company to construct these lines with capital of £45,000 in £10 shares with a £2 limit on any one call. The promoters of the railway were named as Messrs. B. P. Shearer, A. Helps, W. H. Stone, E. W. Ricketts and G. Martin.

To add confusion to the Parliamentary Committee, a second railway Bill with the same title, 'BW, B & B Rly', was submitted in the same session promoted by a Mr. Roy. Little is known of this proposal which was essentially similar to the scheme described above, the main differences being the charges for the conveyance of goods and livestock and in the constitution of the directorship of the company. Fortunately, the Committee were saved from having to consider both schemes as the latter was withdrawn following an agreement between Mr. Roy and Mr. Frankish (who had been elected as solicitor and secretary designate of the former scheme). It later transpired that Roy was paid £250 'in discharge of his agreement to withdraw his bill'.

The first recorded meeting of the BW, B & B Rly Company took place on 26th February 1862 at 23 Parliament Street,

1

London, with B. P. Shearer in the chair. Frankish reported that five petitions had been presented against the Bill. These were:

1. The L & SWR
2. The Proprietors of Bursledon Bridge & Roads
3. Owners and Occupiers of property on the line of railway
4. Reverend Philip Lewis and others
5. William Charles Humphreys

A letter was read from Archibald Scott of the L & SWR dated 24th February outlining the terms under which that company would enter into a working agreement with the BW, B & B. It was obvious to the directors that the support of the L & SWR would not be forthcoming while the extension to Bursledon remained before the select committee. The failure in the 1861 sessions of the Petersfield schemes was, as already described, a result of strong opposition from the L & SWR who rose to challenge any possible threat to their monopoly in South-ampton with its lucrative traffic. It is probable that the risk of any future extension from Bursledon, coupled to the little company being encouraged by the LB & SCR to gain a foot-hold in Southampton, was the prevailing influence upon their actions.

An offer was thus made to withdraw railways Nos. 2 & 3 if the L & SWR would discontinue its opposition. Helps, on presenting this offer, met with a favourable response and was able to enter into discussions to secure better terms for working the line and arrangements for possible purchase. Frankish was able to report in March that the revised Bill had been before Committee in the House of Commons and that all the petitions against it had been withdrawn and it was therefore unopposed.

The title of the company was changed to the 'Bishops Waltham Railway Company' in preparation for the Bill's third reading in the House of Commons on 8th May. In anticipation of a successful conclusion, Mr. John Collister (recently appointed as Engineer) commenced a line survey and the preparation of working plans, whilst a public meeting to be held at the Crown Hotel, Bishops Waltham, was arranged for the 12th May 1862. This was deemed necessary 'to receive information as to the steps which have been taken towards procuring railway accommodation for the district, and to con-sider the best means of accomplishing so desirable an object'. The *Hampshire Advertiser*, in reporting the events of the meeting, referred to 'a numerous and influential attendance, a novel feature in a meeting of this sort being the presence of a large number of ladies'.

Shearer, who chaired the meeting, at once extolled the ben-efits of railway facilities to the district around Bishops Waltham. He continued that they 'had strived constantly to obtain a railway but the attempts had for the most part either failed, or been withdrawn, though at last there seemed every probability of success'. He went on to state that 'For some years past we have been watching the formation of the Mid-Sussex Railway (the LB & SCR branch from Petworth to Midhurst) hoping that some connecting link would be brought from Petersfield to Waltham. The fate of the proposed extension of the Midhurst to Petersfield line, brought before the House of Commons two years ago, had surprised everybody in that neighbourhood looking at the evidence which was produced, but had it been projected to Botley only instead of Southampton, it might perhaps have been carried.'

Shearer then turned attention to the present railway.

'There remained, however, the line which was projected to start from Bursledon, and passing through Botley to Waltham. Gentle-men of commercial views and acquainted with railway oper-ations thought it would be better that the line should start from some place where there was good waterside accommodation, and it was well known that below the bridge at Bursledon, 60 or 80 years ago, 80-gun men-of-war were constructed, and, Bursledon possessing this accommodation, it was proposed that the line should commence there. Several residents south of Botley and between that place and Bursledon, however, objected to that part of the line, and there being no wish, on the part of the promoters, to carry it south of Botley unless with the consent of the landowners, they withdrew that part of the scheme which referred to the south side of the present Botley station, and all opposition to the northern part of the line was withdrawn in return. The bill passed the third reading in the House of Commons on Thursday unopposed, on Friday it was introduced into the House of Lords, and there was every prospect that in the course of a month or so it would receive the Royal assent. He then proceeded to give the heads of the bill. The line would start from the north side of the present Botley station, and would terminate in a field on the western side of the pond at Waltham, its length being three miles and three quarters. The capital was to be £16,000 in 1600 shares of £10 each, with powers to borrow £5000. The first directors of the company, who would remain in office till August next, were himself, Mr. Stone, of Leigh Park; Mr. A. Helps; and Mr. E. W. Ricketts. The line was to be completed within three years, and the tolls were to be the same as upon the South Western Railway, power being reserved for its being worked by that company. The officers of the company at present were Mr. Frankish, a well-known solicitor and par-liamentary agent in London, and Mr. Collister, who was also well known as an engineer of high repute. Only a single line of rails would be laid down in the first instance, but sufficient land would be taken to admit of its being made a double line whenever it was found expedient to do so. All the works would be of the most permanent character. For the accommodation of those who lived halfway between Waltham and Botley there would be a siding for the conveyance of chalk to their clay land. The South-Western Company had undertaken to work the line for 45 per cent. of the gross receipts, and with the option of purchasing the line at cost price, at any time within seven years. He then entered into a consideration of the probable returns, showing that the line might be expected to yield, at least 4 per cent. on the outlay. He assured them he should not have entered into the undertaking but that he deemed it a good investment, and he thought the liberal terms which they had obtained from the South-Western Company were alone sufficient to inspire confidence. About a quarter of the entire capital had been already subscribed.

'Mr. HELPS said that district was very deeply indebted to Mr. Shearer for the interest he had manifested in this undertaking and the support which he gave it. This line had the advantage of not being saddled with the great expense which arose from contests. He had known as much as £10,000 a mile expended on a railway in law costs before the works could be commenced. Having been one of the promoters deputed to negotiate with the South-Western directors he was able to bear testimony to the reasonable manner in which they were met by those parties, and the liberal terms they gave them. He then dwelt upon the general advantages of railway communication, and humorously referring to the present torpid state of Bishop's Waltham, urged them to take shares in the under-taking, which would have the effect of improving the town and increasing the prosperity of the inhabitants.

'The CHAIRMAN explained the route of the projected line, which he said would cross the Winchester road near the ruins, just beyond what is generally known as the boathouse. They might have noticed a small building just on the other side of the pond, at the right

SIR ARTHUR HELPS, K.C.B.

hand of which the station would be placed. The station would be most conveniently situated for passengers.

'Mr. COLLISTER, the engineer, said the line was free from any engineering difficulties, and it might be easily completed in six months from the commencement of the works.

'Mr. WHITEHURST said the coal traffic alone on the line would suffice to pay the interest on the capital, whilst the cheaper rate at which coals could be obtained, in consequence of the railway, would be a great benefit to the poor inhabitants of the town. It would also enable the farmers to obtain lime and draining tiles at a less cost than now, which would be an advantage to them, and tend to the improvement of the land in that locality, much of which was at present in a very bad condition.

'Mr. GUNNER proposed a resolution to the effect that this meeting having heard the explanations furnished by the directors of the Bishop's Waltham Railway, views with satisfaction the prospects of the increased railway accommodation that will be afforded to the neighbourhood, and desires to recommend it to the cordial support of the inhabitants of Bishop's Waltham and the adjoining districts. He said the railway would be of so much advantage to them that they ought, without exception, to give it their best support. For the last half century Bishop's Waltham had stood still whilst other towns in the neighbourhood had progressed, and as they had now a chance of increasing the prosperity of the place, he hoped it would not be neglected.

'Mr. CLARK seconded the resolution, which was then put, and carried unanimously.

'A vote of thanks to the chairman terminated the proceedings.'

Frankish was thus able to report a successful outcome to the directors on the 21st May, by which time subscriptions on capital had reached £4,280, most of this money having been guaranteed by the BWR directors and the Clay Company. Some caution on the part of the directors seems to have prevailed, despite the natural euphoria in Bishops Waltham, as it was resolved to approach the L & SWR for part of the capital. The L & SWR were not too keen to risk their money on this venture and declined, but offered to forego their right to purchase the line within 7 years as specified under the terms of the Agreement and limit it to 3 years instead.

When the Bishops Waltham Railway Act finally received the Royal Assent on the 17th July 1862, events naturally proceeded with a new impetus. Collister and Frankish were formally appointed as Company Engineer and Solicitor & Secretary respectively. Compulsory purchase orders for the land required and notices to quit were sent out. The search for a suitable contractor to build the line had in fact started in May when Collister had made overtures to Rowland Brotherhood, although by July negotiations were taking place with Messrs. Rilson and Ridley who had already submitted a tender pending the results of discussions with the BW Company.

Shearer was in favour of letting the works to Rilson and Ridley on the terms of an amended tender resulting from the negotiations held, but an interesting development deferred this decision. Bircham, the Secretary of the L & SWR, apparently quite suddenly, wrote to Shearer stating that he would bring the Bishops Waltham Railway to the attention of his Board and propose that they construct the line themselves. Knowing the L & SW Co.'s fear of underhand tactics in particular by the LB & SCR, Frankish seized the opportunity to reply:

'My Dear Bircham,
    Pray bring the subject of the Bishops Waltham Railway again under the notice of the L.S.W.R. Board.
    It is clear they cannot let that little spur of railway go into other hands and therefore it is important to them that it should be made at a reasonable expense . . .
    . . . if the L.S.W.R. Board will undertake to complete and open the line before 1863, I have no doubt that the Bishops Waltham Company will fall in with any reasonable terms proposed by your Board.'

Despite the interest shown initially by Bircham, the LSW Board were not inclined to undertake the work under these conditions and discussions were once again resumed with Rilson and Ridley in September. At the Board meeting held early in that month, the amended tender from Rilson and Ridley was approved and sealed. The agreement was for £10,000 cash and £6,000 in Lloyds 5% bonds to construct the line in accordance with the plans submitted. (This figure was exclusive of the station at Bishops Waltham.)

Thus the contractors were able to take possession of the land and work began apace, the first payment of £3,167 to Rilson & Ridley being authorised on 31st October.

The subject of the station at Bishops Waltham was now very much on the directors' minds, having first been discussed at the same September meeting. However, as no plans were yet available from Collister, further discussions were deferred until December when Collister recommended a temporary station in the first instance and commencement of a permanent structure in March. He submitted his plan for the proposed station and suggested that with Mr. Helps' consent, the company should continue the excavation for a line right up to the Chalk Pit. This would allow for the earth to be taken and used for forming the station, to save the cost of purchasing land for the cutting. Helps was happy with this arrangement providing the line was laid out to his approval and that the company provide him with a siding at Lodge farm crossing and another to

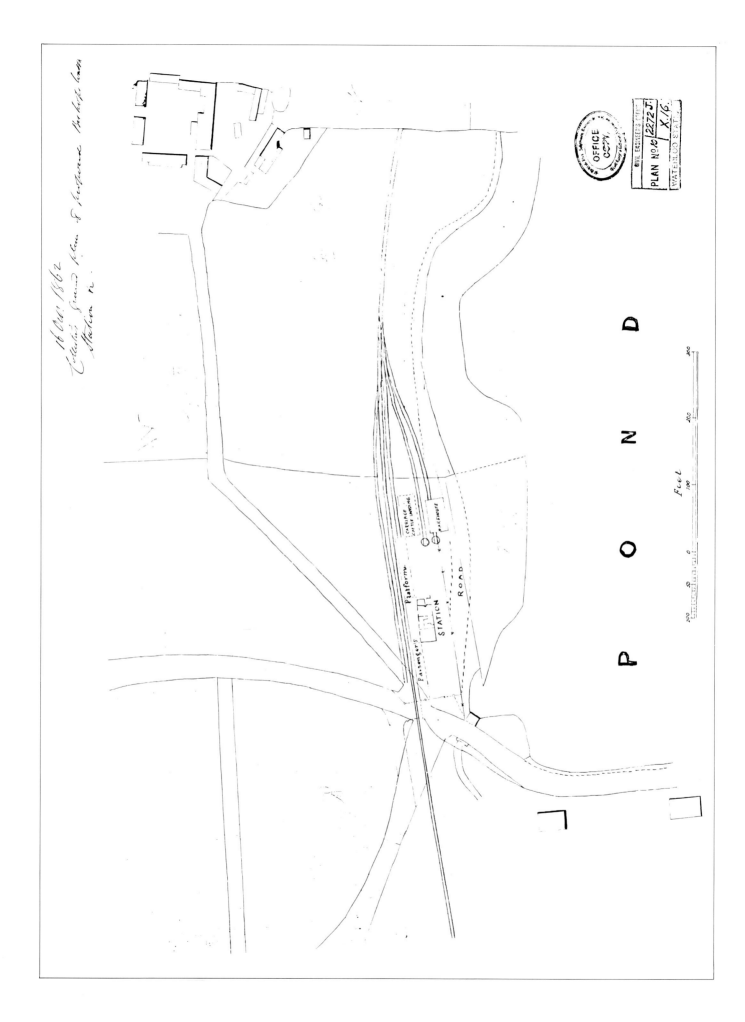

communicate with the works of the Bishops Waltham Clay Company.

The cost of providing the station was estimated at £4,400 exclusive of land which was to be purchased from Mr. Helps for £1,229 (1,200 in shares). A further payment of £5,206 to Rilson and Ridley meant the BW Co. had, by December, expended half of its capital. It had now reached a point where it was becoming necessary for the company to exercise its borrowing powers and an extraordinary meeting of the share-holders was duly called for this purpose for the 22nd December 1862 where approval was given to borrow on mortgage £5,000 on terms determined by the directors. Frankish was instructed to give the requisite notices for a Bill in Parliament seeking an increase in the authorised capital of the company and the sale or lease of the line to the L & SWR. The latter company had made its intention known to the BWR that it would be seeking powers to purchase or leave the line in the ensuing Par-liamentary Sessions. Discussions between the two companies continued until February 1863 after which the L & SWR seem to have lost interest as the subject hardly appears in the minute books.

The BW directors must have been full of optimism when at the first ordinary shareholders meeting, held at the Crown Hotel on the 28th February, they were able to announce an advanced state of the construction of the line. Collister was able to report that:

'The whole of the works are now nearly completed with the excep-tion of the trimming of the slopes and ballasting of the permanent road. The contractors have made arrangements with the engineer of the South-Western company for supplying them with gravel for ballasting from Bishopstoke and I have no doubt but that the line will be so far completed by the end of next month that heavy traffic may pass along.'

By the end of 1862, expenditure of some £10,159 12s 2d had been incurred by the BWR against receipts of £15,158 on account of shares and debentures. In presenting the accounts it was announced that the Bill for authorising an increase in capital was 'in progress', this being essential to facilitate the completion of Bishops Waltham station and the junction with the L & SWR at Botley.

In March 1863 a change of chairman and deputy of the BWR took place when Shearer and Helps did not seek re-election and William Stone and Theodore Martin replaced them. This change at such a critical time for the BW Company seems rather surprising, but the reasons are not recorded.

With the line so near to completion, in April the Board of Trade were informed of the intention to open the railway for passenger traffic, giving the usual one month's notice which acted as a self-imposed stimulus to the company to resolve the issue of the station at Bishops Waltham. At this time no tenders had been sought for the 'temporary station' and Collister was instructed to submit his plans for tender 'limiting the cost as much as practicable'. On the 8th May it was reported that the tender from Mr. Bull of Southampton was let to build a temporary structure to be completed within a fortnight for £103. However, this cost may have been exceeded as a cheque for £125 was paid to Mr. Bull on the 27th November.

Completion of the temporary station inevitably delayed Captain Rich's inspection for the Board of Trade until 28th May. However, perhaps as a face-saver, the delay was blamed on the L & SWR for their dilatory action in erecting signals at the junction at Botley.

Capt. Rich found little substantially wrong with the works and reported as follows:

Reading
29th May 1863

Sir

I have the honour to report for the information of the Lords of the Committee of Privy Council for Trade that in compliance with your minute of the 15th inst. I yesterday inspected the Bishops Waltham Railway which extends from Botley Station on the London and South Western Railway to the Town of Bishops Waltham.

A letter to me from the Secretary, stating that the line would not be ready for inspection till the 25th May was the cause of my postponing the inspection.

The new line is single throughout, with sidings at Botley Station and at Bishops Waltham – land has been purchased for a double line. There are 6 ft. intervals between the lines of rails where there are sidings.

The gauge is 4 ft. 8½. The rail is double headed in lengths of 21 ft. and weighs 75 lbs. per lineal yard. It is fixed in joint chairs weighing 33 lbs. each and with Elm Keys. The chairs are spiked to the sleepers which are laid transversely 3 ft. 6 in apart. The sleepers are 9 ft. long 10 in × 5 and 9 in. × 4½. The ballast is partly chalk partly gravel, laid about 10 in. deep under the sleepers. There are no works of any consequence. Three under bridges of small span have cast iron girders. All the bridges appear to be well and substantially constructed. There are no Engine turntables but as the line is only about four miles long, they might be dispensed with, on condition that Tank Engines only are used.

There is one public level crossing at Bishops Waltham Station.

The following additions are required, and the Engineer has promised that they shall be attended to at once and completed before the line is opened.

A Station Signal and stop buffers at Botley.

Indicators to the facing points at Bishops Waltham and Botley. Clock at Bishops Waltham.

A blind Siding at the latter Station to catch waggons on the goods branch to Bishops Waltham works and prevent them from running through the Station should they get away down the 1 in 60 incline from the works.

The rail to be fished all round the 11 Ch curve approaching Botley Station and on the under bridges.

Some packing and regulating to the line generally, more par-ticularly round the curves. This line not being fished and having many curves should not be worked at great speed. There is no junction for passengers with the London and South Western Railway at Botley. The passengers are to be deposited, on an intervening platform.

I enclose an undertaking as to the proposed mode of working; which appears satisfactory, but a further one, to work with Tank Engines only, is required, when the latter is received, the line can be opened for passenger traffic without danger, but till such an undertaking is reserved, I beg to submit that the Bishops Waltham Railway cannot be opened for passenger traffic without danger to the public using the same by reason of the incompleteness of the works in regard to turntables.

I have etc.
(Signed) T. H. Rich
Capt. R. E.

With time running out, the BWR wasted no time in pro-viding the required indemnity. Frankish, in a letter to the Board of Trade dated 30th May affirmed:

'I am instructed by the Directors of the Bishops Waltham Railway Company to undertake that tank engines only shall be used on the Bishops Waltham Railway until turntables have been placed on the line.'

THE BISHOP'S WALTHAM RAILWAY

WILL BE OPENED FOR TRAFFIC ON MONDAY, 1st JUNE, 1863.

TIME TABLE ON AND AFTER MONDAY, 1st JUNE, 1863, UNTIL FURTHER NOTICE.

Trains to BISHOP'S WALTHAM from LONDON, &c.

	On Week Days.									On Sundays.		
			Exp.				Exp.					
	1 2 3	1 2	1 2	1 2	1 2	1 2	1 2 3	1 2	1 2 3	1 2	1 2 3	1 2
	class.	class.	class.	class.	a.m.	p.m.	class.	class.	p.m.	a.m.	class.	class.
Leave London	a.m.	a.m.	a.m.	a.m.			p.m.	p.m.		a.m.		
Waterloo Bridge Station ...	6 15	8 0	10 40	10 15	11 0	1 10	3 0	4 10	5 0	9 15	10 15	...
" Kensington Station ...	6 10	7 25	9 35	...	...	1 32	...	4 34	...	10 0	...	...
" Kingston ...	6 54	8 21	10 15	...	1 56	...	5 4	...	10 50	11 6	...	
" Woking ...	7 38	10 50	11 3	...	2 13	5 22	5 56		11 34			
" Farnborough ...	8 10	8 55	11 20	...	2 48	5 57	6 30		12 16			
" Basingstoke...	8 52	9 20	11 55	12 15	4 15	4 10	6 40	7 5	12 16	1 0		
" Winchester...	9 36	9 54	12 37	12 50	4 50	5 12		7 35	1 25			
" Bishopstoke ...	10 12			1 12	3 50	5 24	7 35		1 51			
Arr. Botley ...	10 24			1 24	4 0		7 47					
Leave Botley ...	10 30			1 30	4 5	5 30	7 52		1 55			
Arrive Bishop's Waltham ...	10 42			1 42	4 15	5 42	8 4		2 7			

Through Tickets issued from London to Ryde and Cowes via Stokes Bay, inclusive of all charges.

From BISHOP'S WALTHAM to LONDON, &c.

	On Week Days.								On Sundays.	
	Exp.			Exp.						
	1 2	1 2	1 2 3	1 2	1 2	1 2	1 2		a.m.	p.m.
	a.m.	a.m.	a.m.	a.m.	p.m.	p.m.	p.m.			
Trains leave Bishop's Waltham ...	8 15	11 5	11 5	2 30	4 25	6 45			9 0	5 30
Arrive Botley ...	8 27	11 17	11 17	2 42	4 37	6 57			9 10	5 40
Leave Botley ...	8 35	11 25	12 20	2 51	4 48	7 5			9 19	5 49
Arrive Bishopstoke ...	8 46	11 37	12 35	3 5	5 0	7 17			9 31	6 1
" Winchester ...	9 8	12 0	1 15	3 30	5 35	7 47			9 55	6 30
" Basingstoke...	9 45	12 50	2 20	4 10	6 15	8 29			10 55	7 11
" Farnborough ...	10 25	1 22	3 0	4 40	6 40	8 59			11 27	7 45
" Woking ...	10 44	1 44	3 25	5 3		9 20			11 45	8 10
" Kingston ...	11 38	2 31	4 5	5 47		9 30			12 10	8 35
" Kensington ...	12 15		4 57	6 31		10 2			12 37	9 0
" Waterloo Bridge, London ...	11 0	2 30	4 45	5 50	7 35	10 5				

Through Tickets issued from Ryde and Cowes to London via Stokes Bay.

To SOUTHAMPTON, DORCHESTER, WEYMOUTH, SALISBURY, PORTSMOUTH, GOSPORT, &c., from BISHOP'S WALTHAM.

	On Week Days.						On Sundays.	
	a.m.	a.m.	a.m.	p.m.	p.m.	p.m.	a.m.	p.m.
Trains leave Bishop's Waltham ...	8 15	10 0	11	2 30	4 25	6 45	9 0	5 30
Arr. Botley ...	8 27	10 12	11 17	2 42	4 37	6 57	9 10	5 40
Leave Botley ...	8 35		11 25	2 51	4 48	7 5	9 19	5 49
Arr. Bishopstoke ...	8 46		11 37	3 5	5 0	7 17	9 31	6 1
" Southampton	9 55		12 0	3 30	5 20	7 50	9 55	6 20
" Ringwood ...	11 42		2 21		6 20	8 37	2 59	
" Wimborne ...	12 0		2 40		6 39	8 54	3 19	
" Blandford ...	12 36		3 18		7 15	9 48	4 9	
" Dorchester ...	1 3		3 42		7 37		4 23	
" Weymouth ...	1 28		4 0		8 0	10 5	4 45	
Leave Bishopstoke ...	9 10		11 55	3 50	5 10	7 35	9 47	8 10
Arr. Romsey ...	9 26		12 11	4 5	5 25	7 45	10 10	8 25
" Salisbury ...	10 0		12 47	4 40	6 0	8 25	10 50	9 5
Leave Botley ...								
Arr. Fareham ...	10 24	12 7	10 55	3 25	5 24	7 47	10 18	1 37
" Gosport ...	10 36	12 19		3 35	5 32	7 59	10 30	1 49
" Stokes Bay ...	10 47	12 35	10 55	3 46	5 47	8 10		2 8
" Porchester ...			11	3 55	5 49		10 26	1 56
" Cosham ...	10 50	12 33		3 49	5 50	8 13	10 33	2 1
" Portsmouth ...	11	0 12 50		4 0	6 0	8 25	10 55	2 15

FROM WEYMOUTH, DORCHESTER, SOUTHAMPTON, PORTSMOUTH, GOSPORT, SALISBURY, &c., TO BISHOP'S WALTHAM.

	On Week Days.					On Sundays.	
	a.m.	a.m.	p.m.	p.m.	p.m.	a.m.	p.m.
Leave Weymouth ...	8 0	11 40	12 20	2 15	4 50	6 15	
" Dorchester ...	8 10	11 50	12 45	2 25	5 15	6 40	
" Blandford ...	8 15	11 56	12 55	2 30	5 15	6 50	
" Wimborne ...	7 55	10 50	1 36	4 10	5 57	7 55	
" Ringwood ...	7 29	9 56	1 55	4 20	6 13	7 55	
" Southampton	6 30	7 44	10 15	1 55	4 50	6 15	7 30
Arrive Bishopstoke ...	6 45	9 45	12 45	3 0	5 5	9 30	1 15
Leave Salisbury ...		7 55	11 40	2 15	4 15	8 33	
Arrive Bishopstoke ...		8 50	12 35	3 0	5 5	9 40	
Leave Portsmouth ...	8 0	11 40	12 40	2 15	4 15	6 30	
" Cosham ...	8 10	11 50	12 50	2 25	4 25	6 40	
" Porchester ...	8 15	11 56	2 15	2 30	6 46		
" Stokes Bay ...	7 55	10 50	1 10	4 10	6 20	6 55	
" Gosport ...	8 5	11 50	1 30	4 20	6 40	8 55	
" Fareham ...	8 24	12 41	1 38	4 41	6 55	9 7	
Arrive Botley ...	8 35	12 20	2 51	2 51	7 5	9 19	
Leave Bishopstoke ...	6 48	10 12	1 12	3 15	5 12	9 45	1 25
Arrive Botley ...	7 0	10 24	1 24	3 25	5 24	10 20	1 51
Leave Botley ...	8 40	10 30	1 30	4 5	5 30	10 25	1 55
Arrive Bishop's Waltham ...	8 52	10 42	1 42	4 15	5 42	10 37	2 7

By Order,

ARCHD. SCOTT, Traffic Manager.

WATERLOO BRIDGE STATION,
LONDON, June, 1863.

CHAPTER TWO
'HOPE AND DESPAIR'
1863 to 1881

ON the 1st June 1863 the town of Bishops Waltham was *en fête* to celebrate the opening of the line. The *Hampshire Telegraph* reported on the 6th June:

'The Bishops Waltham Railway was opened for public traffic on Monday last, which made the little town full of bustle and life. The beautiful toned bells of the old parish church were ringing a merry peel the whole day, and a celebrated brass band paraded the town; the Bishops Waltham Rifle Band also assisted. The principal gentlemen and tradesmen met at the Crown Hotel to inaugurate the opening of the railway. About fifty sat down to a first class dinner, served up by Mr. Pratt to the satisfaction of all present, the wines being first rate.

'A. Helps Esq. occupied the chair, Mr. Wyatt filling the vice chair. The first toasts were proposed by Mr. Helps 'The Queen, Prince and Princess of Wales and all the Royal Family', which were cordially responded to. Other toasts followed and were responded to by Mr. Ricketts, Dr. Parry, Dr. Greaves, Mr. Blanchford, Mr. Wyatt, Mr. Bond, Mr. Verseman and Mr. Whitney who represented the South-Western Railway Company. The proceedings were kept up with great spirit to a late hour, everyone present appearing delighted. The day's proceedings concluded with the band playing God Save the Queen.'

With one-engine-in-steam working six trains in each direction were provided on weekdays, with three workings on Sundays (see timetable on page 6).

The BW Co. were now keen to complete the permanent facilities at Bishops Waltham, the directors resolving that the foundations for the passenger station be 'got in' as soon as possible. By August this work was in progress and in addition the contract for the goods shed had been let to Rilson & Ridley who had tendered for £700. However, sub-soil problems were experienced with the sites of both these structures. So in October it was determined that the station house should be constructed in wood and Taylor's patent face bricks instead of a conventional brick building as originally approved and the goods shed was completely re-sited (the original intended location is shown on page 4). It was therefore February 1864 before Collister could report that the goods shed and sidings were nearly ready and that the passenger station was 'far advanced', and it would appear from the minute books that further delays were experienced, as it was stated at the shareholders meeting on 31st August 1864 that 'The necessary buildings for accommodating passengers and goods at Bishops Waltham are now nearly completed.'

Regardless of the obvious problems, the delays to the new station may have been simply the inability to raise the additional capital of £8,000 authorised on 22nd June 1863 to complete the works. The facilities were finally opened for public traffic in March or April 1865.

The announcement by the promoters of a proposed railway from Petersfield to Bishops Waltham was greeted with a cautious neutrality by the BW directors, the company being cognisant of the attitude of the L & SWR towards such an extension. Frankish reported on 26th June 1863 that he had corresponded with Bircham of the latter company to ascertain whether the South-Western would object to the BWR seeking what support they could obtain towards such a scheme and recommending that the L & SWR should undertake the construction themselves. Predictably, a rather curt response was forthcoming, 'the [LSW] company does not deem any extension to Petersfield necessary'. In the light of this obvious hostility, the directors resolved on 29th December to lodge a petition against the Bill for 'the protection of the Company'. A similar reaction was also given to the proposed extension of the Alton, Alresford & Winchester Railway from Ropley to Fareham via Hambledon and Droxford (later amended by an Act of 29th July 1864 truncating the line by forming a junction with the proposed Petersfield & Bishops Waltham line at Mconstoke).

However, by May 1864 it appears the LSWR had reached an agreement with the P & BWR as they withdrew their opposition. This gave the BWR the opportunity to come out and openly support the P & BWR Bill. They, in turn, withdrew their opposition upon what seems to have been a vague and face-saving agreement with the P & BWR promoters to 'restrict their rights of interference with the property of the Bishops Waltham Railway'. With the effective opposition thus withdrawn, the P & BWR Act was passed on 29th July 1864 with a capital of £150,000.

At the ordinary general meeting of the shareholders on the 31st August, the company were of the view that:

'An Act had been passed during the last session of Parliament authorising the construction of a new line of Railway from Bishops Waltham to Petersfield and your directors have no doubt that the completion of this line will materially add to the traffic over your railway.'

The first traffic returns of the BWR had been fairly modest (see Appendix 6) revealing a small profit to the company upon deduction of working expenses. The receipts from goods traffic has arisen chiefly from the Bishops Waltham Clay Co. although this firm had not been in full production at least for the latter half of the year.

Although the directors could not recommend a dividend on ordinary shares, they boldly concluded that:

'The large and rapid development of the town of Bishops Waltham leaves little room for doubt that a renumerative amount of traffic will ultimately be brought over the line.'

Indeed, everyone concerned with the little company cannot have imagined the series of disasters which were to beset it over the next few years.

Arthur Ricketts had resigned his seat as a director in May owing to the fact that he 'had parted with a great number of shares in the Clay Co.'. The close working relationship between the two companies can be gleaned by the fact that three other directors of the BWR, Helps, Martin and Moore, held similar positions with the BWCC. Helps was also on the board of the newly formed Bishops Waltham Gas and Coke Company

Clay Pit

D.W.

Clay Pit

307

Clay Pit

**Bishop's Waltham
Clay Works**
328

329

Gasometer

315

314

Clay Pit

327

341

316

Clayland Cottages

317

164

326

342

3

Victoria Buildings

312

Foresters Arms
(P.H.)

318

14.9

322

325

323

324

Saw Mills
(Steam)

Timber Yard

343

Bisho

320

324

188

British Schools
(Boys & Girls)

491

493

VICTORIA

Railway

ROAD

492

S.P.

B.M. 122.8

495

Boat House

An extract from the 25 inch Ordnance Survey of 1870 showing the
station and surroundings. Of interest is the siding arrangement and
tramway in the brickworks. Later surveys show the Gas Works
siding shortened to the approach cutting. The siding below the
public level crossing led to a slaughterhouse located on the west side
of the line but little more is known as this was removed by as early
as 1900.

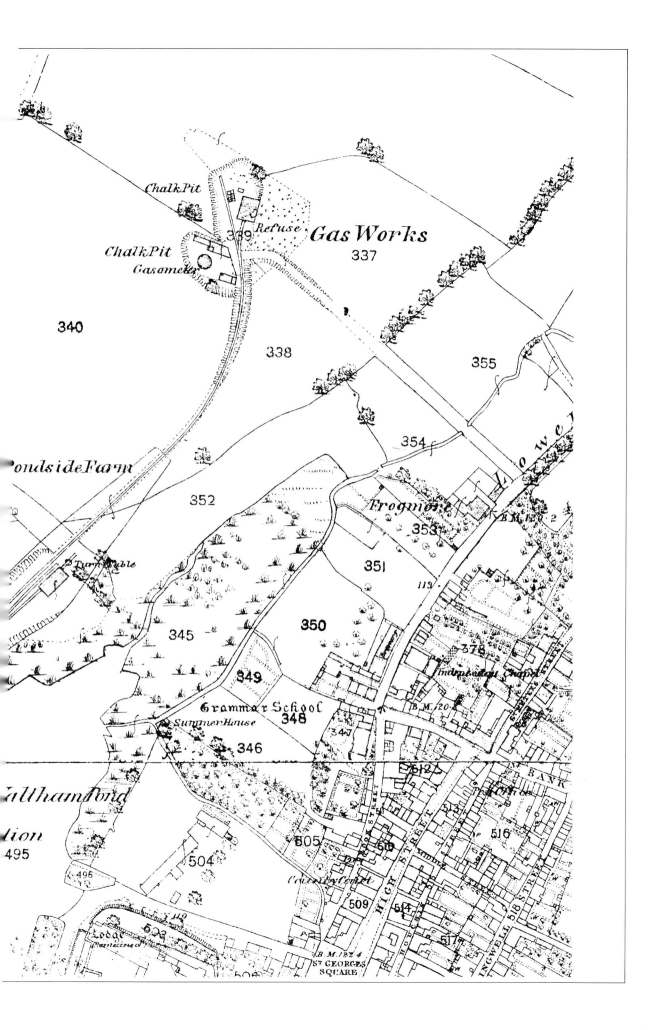

which had commenced production in March 1864. This company had rented land near to the clay workings from Helps at a nominal rent of £5 p.a. for 200 years. An agreement was made between the Clay and Gas Companies for the latter to take over the private siding. Frankish, who also acted as solicitor and secretary for the Gas Co., was able to arrange for Rilson & Ridley to clear and prepare the site for £25.

The state of the money market in 1865 seriously impaired the ability of the promoters of the P & BWR to raise capital for their line. It was reported to the BWR directors in August that:

> 'The works on the line from Bishops Waltham to Petersfield have not yet commenced, but it is understood that negotiations for letting them are pending.'

The economic depression was also having an effect upon the BWR as receipts for the two years from the opening had been disappointing. The first half of 1865 had revealed a drop in traffic compared to 1864 with gross receipts down significantly and the second half improving only by a small margin (see Appendix 6). There was no question of any dividend being paid to the shareholders who were informed at the half-yearly meeting on the 28th February 1866:

> 'The delay in commencing the construction of the Bishops Waltham and Petersfield line has of course tended to retard the development of traffic on your railway, but it is hoped that when the money market becomes easier the works will be undertaken.'

The directors must have been profoundly disappointed with the situation. The early promise and euphoria of 1863 had been sharply jolted by the circumstances now prevailing and the failure of the P & BW was not the only setback. The Clay Company, one of the main sources of traffic to the line, had diminished considerably in the mid–1860s as demand for their products contracted to the point where production had all but ceased. The cattle plague which had broken out in southern Hampshire, coupled to the reduction in importance of Botley Market owing to the establishment of the large central Market at Southampton, also took its toll.

Despite the lack of income, prospective creditors were of course placing demands upon the BW Company. Mr. Taylor, the company's architect, who had requested payment of £211 19s 0d in February 1865 for his services, was refused by the directors owing to the 'inability of the Company from want of funds to discharge it'. He was offered preference shares in lieu of the amount owed, but this was declined! By May, Taylor was pressing again and the directors finally resolved to foot the bill out of their own pockets to 'meet the emergency'.

A recommendation from the LSWR in January 1866 urging the erection of an engine shed at Bishops Waltham met with the same response. The directors informed the LSW that they had no funds available to build a shed, but they were prepared to pay interest on the cost of the LSWR erecting such a structure. The provision of an engine shed had been included in Collister's plans of August 1863 for the new station, but was not proceeded with. A cost of £500 for a shed was eventually agreed between the companies in July, the BWR paying 6% interest, but for reasons not recorded the work was not undertaken.

A degree of optimism was possible, however, with the prospect of the opening of the works of the South of England Wagon Company. The shareholders were informed in August 1865:

> 'The South of England Waggon Company has recently been formed and having selected a site for their works at the Bishops Waltham end of the line, their operations must increase the traffic upon it.'

An application for a siding from the firm had been received on 8th April 1865, and after consulting the LSWR an agreement for working and maintenance was made between the BWR and the Wagon Co. The LSW constructed the siding with the BW Company paying interest at $7\frac{1}{2}\%$. It is believed to have been located on the west side south of the level crossing and some 448 yards in length. Evidence from Ordnance Surveys and Official Plans suggest that it had been removed by 1900.

Other new works carried out at this time were the provision of a crane at Bishops Waltham for £110 following requests from the LSWR, Collister and the Botley station master early in 1865. Following more appeals from the South Western, a water column was installed and paid for by that company, the BWR undertaking to pay for it at valuation 'on expiry of the existing agreement.'

The year 1866 witnessed what was to be the final publication of the Company's capital account to 30th June which only amplifies the predicament the Company had reached:

Receipts		Expenditure	
Total amounts received	£34,480.0.0.	Amounts expended on works	£35,297.6.4.
Balance £	817.6.4.		
	£35,297.6.4.		£35,297.6.4.

With many unpaid debts and little hope of adequate income to settle the creditor's claims, the BWR were faced with a claim by Ridley, one of the contract partners. He had signed an Action against the company for £2,371 17s 10d (later amended to £2,389 15s 10d), principle and interest on four of his Lloyds Bonds in January 1866. The directors, having little choice, resolved not to defend the Action, allowing judgement to go by default which Ridley signed in February.

The shareholders were informed at the half-yearly meeting in August:

> 'Mr. Ridley one of the Contractors for the line prior to the 1st June last, commenced proceedings against the company to obtain a preference over the other conditions and prevent the profits arising from the Bishops Waltham line being handed over to your Directors, and he has since obtained an Order of the Court of Chancery for the sale of the line. Your Directors have every reason to believe that the proceedings which Mr. Ridley has taken have acted very prejudicially against the Company as respects negotiations into which they were entering for the sale of the line to the South Western Company.'

The subject of the sale to the LSWR had been discussed again in July when it was reported at the Directors meeting on the 11th that:

> 'negotiations had been progressing with the South Western Company for the purchase of the Bishops Waltham line and the terms to be asked and taken'

Frankish informed the Directors in August that Ridley's Bill

> 'they can only attribute to the various causes that have operated to a similar lessening of traffic on so many of the larger lines.'

The inevitable pruning of costs became paramount and with effect from the introduction of the summer timetables, the Sunday service was completely withdrawn and the weekday mid-afternoon train was taken off (see Appendix 8), leaving five trains in each direction.

If recent events weren't setback enough, the BWR Co was about to plunge into a desperate and unthinkable state of affairs. In April the Bishops Waltham Clay Company finally went into liquidation, trading being carried on by the liquidators until December when the final trickle of production ceased. The consequent loss of revenue to the BWR was felt instantly with half-yearly goods receipts falling to a paltry £189 13s 4d (see Appendix 6). Only two months before the bankruptcy, at the General Meeting on 28th February, shareholders were being informed:

'negotiations are pending with reference to the Bishops Waltham Clay Works, which they hope may result in there being more activity carried on than before and increasing the traffic on the line.'

The directors meeting on 6th May 1867 turned out to be one of the most eventful in the short history of the company. Frankish, having referred to the prosecution of Ridley's Chancery Suit, reported that Rilson, the other contractor partner, had served a writ against the BWR Co. for £3,204 10s 0d (Lloyds Bonds of £2,950 plus interest). Frankish continued by announcing that his own amount of unpaid bills of costs up to the end of 1866 amounted to £1,938 9s 7d and 'being desirous of obtaining a judgement against the Company forthwith proposed to commence an action for this amount'. He then placed before the directors an account from Collister for bills totalling £794 2s 6d, the balance due for his services. He, too, intended to obtain a judgement against the company. With no prospect of any revenue to settle these claims, the directors resolved that these actions would not be defended.

In August the luckless shareholders were informed of the wretched state of affairs. The millstone of mounting debts and the increasing queue of creditors were revealed to the proprietors, most of whom must have given up any hope of ever receiving a return on their investment. The chairman reported that 'In consequence of the Chancery proceedings by Mr. Ridley against the company the South Western Company pay over no part of the receipts'. As a result, no half-yearly statement of accounts was produced as they 'are not altered from the statement and Balance sheet submitted and sent to the shareholders at the last half yearly meeting'.

With no prospect of the commencement of the P & BWR during 1867 owing to the continued depressed state of the money market, an application for abandonment was made in March 1868 by the secretary for the company to the Board of Trade. It was the company's view that:

'The entire loss of public confidence in new railway companies as an investment for Capital has rendered it quite hopeless to attempt to raise the money necessary for the construction of this line'.

Abandonment was sanctioned on 28th July, the company having expended some £2,337, mainly on parliamentary expenses.

By August 1868 the BWR shareholders had become totally in Chancery was filed against both the BW and the LSW Companies to enforce payment in lieu of annual profits and to prevent them being paid over to anyone else by the LSWR. He had also petitioned for the sale of the line. The directors naturally resolved to appeal against the Master of the Rolls' decision ordering a sale of the line.

The *Hampshire Telegraph* reported on 17th November on the resultant hearing:

'In the Court of Chancery on Thursday last an appeal was made from an order of the Master of the Rolls directing an inquiry under the 27th and 28th Vic. Cap. 112 (The Judgement Law Amendment Act 1864) to consider what lands the company has and ordering the same to be sold in satisfaction of the creditors debt. Messrs. Ridley and Ritson the contractors had obtained judgement and execution against the company. The Sherriff returned that the Company had no goods or chattels and that the only land which they had was that upon which the railway was made and the stations and good sheds were built. The Company had appealed from the Order of the Master of the Rolls upon the ground that on the face of the return, it appeared that the Company had no lands which could be sold for the payment of the creditors debt. It appeared that the Company had entered into an agreement with the South Western Railway Company to work the railway for a certain number of years.

'Mr. Jessel and Mr. Fitzhugh for the Company contended that the Company were bound to maintain and work the railway for the benefit of the public, that they had no saleable interest in the land and that the Order for the sale was inoperative. As it manifestly appeared that the Company had no lands other than those upon which the line was constructed it was useless to go to the expense of an inquiry in Chambers to ascertain whether there were any lands which could be sold to satisfy the judgement.

'Mr. Malis and Mr. Barber for the judgement creditors contended that they were entitled to have a sale of the Company's interest, whatever it might be. That would not interfere with the Working Agreement and the railway would still be maintained and worked for the benefit of the public.

'Lord Justice Turner said that the Judgement Law Amendment Act gave no higher powers as to the lands subject to be taken in execution than the creditor previously possessed. Before that Act was passed their lands could not be taken in execution and were incapable of being sold. The Court could not make an Order for sale unless it was first ascertained whether there were any lands liable to be sold. The Order of the Court, so far as it directed a sale, would be discharged; the rest of the petition would stand over till it was ascertained what lands the Company had liable to be taken in execution.'

The outcome of the Court of Chancery was something of a hollow victory for the BWR as Ridley remained resolute in pressing his claim upon the profits of the company, the effect of which as recorded by Frankish:

'beyond putting himself and the Company to needless expense is that the South Western Company declines to pay any part of the receipts pending the litigation'.

It appears that the 'in limbo' position of the company effectively stopped negotiations with the LSWR over the sale of the line and no further reference to the subject appears in the BWR minute books for the time being. Eventually the date by which the LSW could take up their option of purchase under the 1863 Agreement, the 1st June 1867, was passed.

More gloom was reported to the hapless shareholders in February 1867 when the directors voiced their disappointment at the dwindling returns announced for the latter half of 1866: disillusioned and apathetic to the company's future. Despite the usual notices of the half-yearly meeting to be held on 26th August, no shareholders presented themselves and the meeting had to be adjourned *sine die*.

With the company's affairs effectively suspended, the Board did not sit again until 27th February 1869, a meeting which proved to be as disastrous as that in May 1867. Frankish was not present to report the proceedings and it was announced that he had resigned his position as secretary and that a Mr. Samuel Teed had been elected to the post 'in lieu'. This was only to be expected as Frankish can hardly have been prepared to preside over any further bills with little prospect of settlement.

The meeting continued with Teed presenting letters of resignation from each director. The entire Board, Theodore Martin, Arthur Helps, Alexander Williams, William Stone and John Moore, had collectively resolved that the hopeless situation of the company was irretrievable and they had had enough of the railway's affairs. This unfortunate but not unexpected action has rendered events of the next decade into total obscurity as all financial transactions were held in Chancery. In effect the company remained in a state of suspension. However the L & SWR continued to work the line under the existing agreement and retained all receipts.

An upturn in fortunes for traffic on the line occurred in 1871 when the abandoned Clay Company works were acquired by Mark Henry Blanchard who recommenced production at Bishops Waltham in addition to his London business. A full description of the Clay Company and subsequent history appears in Appendix 1. A general increase in traffic may have been responsible for the introduction by 1873 of an additional return working to provide an extra morning service (See Appendix 8). The population of Bishops Waltham had also increased from 2,267 in 1861 to 2,618 in 1871, but it is difficult at this range in time to judge whether this had any direct effect on traffic.

March 1875 saw the death of Sir Arthur Helps. Although no longer connected with the BWR, his efforts in bringing the railway to the town of Bishops Waltham deserve the highest regard. There is no doubt the BWR would not have existed without Helps and, as with his other enterprises in the town, he left the inhabitants with a legacy for which they owed him a great debt of gratitude.

Despite the difficulty in dealing with the BWR, the L & SW were still mindful of the need for locomotive accommodation at Bishops Waltham. Discussing the matter on 30th January 1876, it was stated that a 'small engine house' could be provided at a cost not exceeding £40. A decision was deferred until the issue was raised again on 22nd March 1877 when revised estimates were submitted for £200 if constructed in brick or £120 if in timber. In the event, the latter was adopted, presumably at the sole expense of the L & SWR.

Matters now rested until 1881 when, on 11th May, Archibald Scott reported to the LSW directors that he had communicated with Ridley in respect of his judgement and efforts to obtain control over the BW company, the latter being described as 'practically non-existent for several years'. The L & WR's intention in the ensuing negotiations was the ultimate purchase of the BWR. Their directors resolved on 5th July to propose to the shareholders at the half-yearly meeting in August that the BWR could be purchased at a probable cost of about £22,000.

It fell to Ralph Dutton on 4th August to explain to the LSW shareholders:

> 'There has been some difficulty in dealing with this Company from the fact that it was in Chancery with no directors, no engineer and no secretary; nothing but a crop of creditors and we had to deal with them the best way we could. However I belive we have got all interests together now as nearly as possible and that the undertaking can be bought up for a sum not exceeding £20,500,

and then, it will come absolutely into our own hands'.

These arrangements met with the satisfaction of the shareholders and they resolved:

> 'that this meeting approves the agreement for the purchase by this Company of the Railways and Undertaking of the Bishops Waltham Railway Company as submitted to the Meeting, and authorises and requests the Directors to complete the same, with any modifications they may think proper and conducive to the interests of this Company'

Negotiations between the L & SW and Ridley had obviously reached an amicable conclusion by September, as a special general meeting was called under the auspices of the Bishops Waltham Railway Company, the notice for which appeared in the *Hampshire Independent* on the 24th September:

> 'Notice is hereby given that in pursuance of the London and South Western Railway Act 1863, a special General Meeting of this Company will be held at the offices of Messrs. Frankish and Buchanan, Deveraux Court, Strand, London on Tuesday the 11th day of October 1881 at 11 o'clock in the forenoon, for the purpose of considering and if thought fit sanctioning the sale of the Railway sidings, Stations, Works and Conveniences, undertaking and property of this Company to the London and South Western Railway Company also for the purpose of electing Directors of the Bishops Waltham Railway Company and of such other proceedings as may be necessary for carrying such a sale into effect.
> Dated this 21st day of September 1881
>
> 　　　　　　　　　　　　　　Samual Teed, Secretary.'

At the subsequent meeting, Samual Coakes Ridley, William Gold Buchanan, William Henry Vause, Rev. Sidney Porter, and Clement Stackhouse Helps were elected as Directors. Those present resolved that:

> 'A sale of all the railway sidings, stations, works, and conveniences, land and properties of the Bishops Waltham Railway Company and all rights and privalges be made therewith to the London and South Western Railway by virtue of the South Western Railway Act 1863 for a sum of not less than £20,000 and that a draft agreement for effecting such a sale be drawn up'.

The L & SW directors gave their approval to the purchase of the line for £20,000 on the 27th October, payment to be arranged by the Finance Committee 'at the proper time'. An unspecified alteration to the Agreement was approved and sealed on 8th December owing to the 'special circumstances' of the BWR Company. A Special General Meeting of the BW Company on the 30th December gave the final authorisation to effect the sale to the L & SWR in retrospect from 4th August 1881.

BWR's era of independence thus drew to a close. Born with hope and confidence and the promise of a rapid development in traffic, some eight years had instead witnessed the BWR struggle through a host of adversities crippling the establishment of the company, leaving it with a millstone of debts, and culminating in the inevitable sell-out. There is no doubt that the decline and ultimate failure of the Clay Company played a major role in retarding the development of traffic in the crucial early years of the railway's existence. Whether enough revenue would have been generated to settle with the mounting list of creditors can only be conjectured, but it seems unlikely. Who can really blame the directors on that day in February 1869 for 'throwing in the towel' given the dire situation? The minute books record the end for the Bishops Waltham Railway Company as 1881, but in reality the concern had effectively disappeared twelve years before.

CHAPTER THREE

'A DEGREE OF RECOVERY'
1881 to 1932

WITH the purchase of the line settled, the L & SW directors resolved in May 1882 to create and issue as ordinary stock the cost of the undertaking, but not to raise additional capital to settle the outstanding debts of the BWR as 'all monies heretofore borrowed by the Bishops Waltham Company have been paid off by this Company out of their purchase money'. The eventual settlement with the BW Company was reported to the directors by Bircham in February as £22,000. This increase may have been linked to the alteration to the Agreement sealed in December.

The new owners lost little time effecting improvements to the timetable. The train service was increased from six to seven workings daily in 1883, with the introduction of a mid-morning service departing Bishops Waltham at 9.50 a.m. completing the return trip from Botley at 10.15 a.m., and the 1884 timetable saw the commencement of a mid-afternoon train to fill the somewhat long gap in the service which had existed since 1867. In 1893 separate daily goods working was introduced, the down train arriving at Bishops Waltham at 8.10 a.m. from Botley, the engine having previously first worked 'light' from the terminus. The return 'up' goods left Bishops Waltham at 5.20 p.m., arriving at Botley at 5.35 p.m.

The train staff and ticket system of working the branch was in July 1897 authorised to be replaced by Tyer's No. 6 train tablet at an estimated cost of £173. This was eventually sanctioned by the Board of Trade on 9th June 1898.

Although not related to the branch, it may be of interest to mention an invention patented by Mark Blanchard Jnr., whose father had purchased the BW Clay Company in 1871. Having an interest in railway matters, his invention was reported in the *Hampshire Telegraph* on 15th January 1887:

'Improvements in Railway Couplings – Mr. Mark Henry Blanchard Jnr. of Bishops Waltham has just patented an invention for improvements in railway couplings, which is calculated to prevent loss of many lives and limbs annually. To the ordinary hook which is fitted to rolling stock a link of U form is fitted by means of a rivet or bolt passing through the open ends of the link and hook respectively. On each side of the link is a lever or crank, by operating upon which the link can be raised or lowered from a vertical to a horizontal position. These cranks are connected with other levers, the ends of which reach to the sides of the vehicles or thereabouts. When two trucks are brought near together an attendant can, by moving one of the levers on either side, lower or raise the link and thereby couple or uncouple the vehicles as desired, without the necessity of going between them. In adapting the invention to locomotive engines and other vehicles where it is desirable to manipulate the coupling from the platform or other position, the levers are modified so that the operation can be carried out without the necessity for the attendant leaving such position.'

A POSSIBILITY OF EXPANSION

With the BW line now in a consolidated position, the L & SW directors were informed on 25th October 1883 that surveys were to be made and notices prepared for a line from Bishops Waltham to Droxford in the next Parliamentary Session.

However, no further mention of this proposal appears until plans were deposited in 1889 for a light railway to run from an end-on junction at Bishops Waltham to Brockbridge (Droxford).

Much to the disappointment of the inhabitants of Bishops Waltham, nothing came of this. An indication of the townspeople's frustration may be gained from a communication sent to the L & SW from the Clerk to the Bishops Waltham Parish Council in August 1896 requesting that any future scheme for new railways in the neighbourhood should arrange for a connection to Bishops Waltham. The prod the L & SW may have needed came in 1899 when a letter was received on 8th May from the Finance Mines and Industries Association stating their intention to promote a light railway under the terms of the existing proposal of 1889 (this time connecting with the now authorised Meon Valley line, forming a junction facing Alton) if the L & SW would give them a junction at both ends of the line. Although this offer was declined, notices nevertheless appeared in the *London Gazette* on 25th May seeking backing for the scheme and stating that Parliamentary approval was to be sought under the Light Railways Act of 1896. Without the necessary junction arrangements with the L & SW both ends of the line would have to connect with a siding.

The application called the Bishops Waltham Light Railway Order 1899 came before the Board of Trade in mid-1899. The proposal was for a line from the existing L & SW line at Bishops Waltham curving north eastwards, crossing the Bishops Waltham to Morestead road and the Bishops Waltham to Alton road, and continued eastwards past Dundridge Farm. A north-westerly direction was then followed south of Shepherds Farm, crossing the Droxford to Winchester road at its intersection with Sheep Pond Lane, the line turning eastwards across Shepherds Down to terminate at a point north of Droxford station after crossing the Fareham to Alton road near the 9 mile post from Fareham. The total length of the proposed line was to be 4 miles 2 furlongs and 8 chains with a ruling gradient of 1 in 50. Estimated costs were shown as £34,793 or about £8,000 per mile with a proposed capital of £45,000 with borrowing powers of £15,000. The engineer was named as H. Michell Whitley.

The Board of Trade inquiry, held at the Institute, Bishops Waltham on Saturday 21st October, heard objections to the new line from: the L & SW on grounds of interference with their stations at Bishops Waltham and Droxford (although they did not object in principle); Mr. Blanchard stating that his facilities would be interfered with; Messrs. Crowley & Co. Brewers who would lose some land; and Droxford Parish Council regarding adequate provision for crossing a road. No other objections were received, the general impression being that the line would have a real agricultural and industrial value. The Commissioners were generally satisfied with the arrangements, although some concern was expressed over the estimated expenditure for earthworks involving some 130,500 cubic yards; with much of the route passing through solid rock,

Bishops Waltham High Street, looking south about 1917. As a flourishing market town and business centre, the town was one of the earliest in the county to boast gas street lighting.
COURTESY JOHN BOSWORTH

Station Road, looking back towards the town c.1906. The buildings in the left foreground are the livery stables, part of which once belonged to the Palace. They probably date from the 14th century. The first building on the right is the old fire engine house.
                                        COURTESY JOHN BOSWORTH

costs were in the order of £2,300 per mile. The capital figure required for the new railway drew terse comment from Sir Courtenay Boyle of the B.O.T.

> '£45,000 is a great deal for a light railway of 4½ miles . . . the Board has doubt whether some of these schemes are light railways at all.'

Confirmation of the BWLR Order was made on 10th May 1900 by the Board of Trade still containing reference to the relative high cost of construction. Col. Yorke also insisted that the siding from which the junction was made at Bishops Waltham would need to be made fit for passenger traffic. The Order was finally signed and sealed by the B.O.T. on 26th October.

Not unexpectedly, the promoters found few individuals prepared to invest money in their venture, like many similar light railway undertakings at this time the number of applications, duplicity and topographic features all played a major part in their being doomed to failure. With hindsight it is fortunate that the BWLR was not built, passing through thinly populated areas it could never have been a success and is unlikely to have justified such a high construction cost.

Another Light Railway proposal surfaced in March 1900 emanating from landowners in the Winchester area for a line from Bishops Waltham to the city, passing through Lower Upham, Fishers Pond, Colden Common and Twyford, with connections to both the LSWR and Didcot, Newbury & Southampton Company's lines south of Winchester. How-

ever, although a Light Railway Order was confirmed in November, no more was heard of the scheme.

Despite the improvements the L & SW had made to the weekday train service on the BWR in the mid 1880s, a large section of residents in the area were unhappy that no Sunday service had been provided since 1866. In August 1889 a widely signed petition was sent to the L & SW requesting a train service on Sundays. It contained several influential leading signatories, one being Sir William Jenner, physician to Queen Victoria.

However, the L & SW directors saw fit to decline both this and a subsequent Memorial for the same request in November. Further changes in train timings in 1900 also proved an unpopular move, resulting in the company receiving petitions and resolutions in July and October of that year, both drawing a negative response from the directors. Despite lack of success, a third attempt was made in March 1901 to persuade the L & SW of the inconvenience of the alterations, this time by a concerted effort from several parish authorities in the neighbourhood. However, the L & SW remained resolute.

On 5th November 1904 a significant move by the L & SW was to lead to great improvements in the service on the branch. The General Manager reported to the directors that owing to insufficient accommodation and lack of ventilation, the steam railmotor cars had been withdrawn from service on the Basingstoke and Alton Light Railway in August. He suggested that the railmotors thus released might be used with advantage on

A superb view of Bishops Waltham soon after the introduction of the steam railmotor service on 10th November 1904. Railmotor No. 1 is simmering in the platform while the station master looks to the camera. The station house was a remarkable building executed in red and yellow bricks around a wooden frame. The chimneys were constructed with horizontal and diagonal chevron patterns using yellow and red bricks with striking effect.
NATIONAL RAILWAY MUSEUM

The local carriers, Sid Rogers and Harry Fielder, in the station forecourt. The Crown Hotel was the agent for parcels, Sid Rogers having two horses which were also used to pull the local fire engine.
COURTESY JOHN BOSWORTH

the Bishops Waltham and Turnchapel branches. This was approved and appears to have been put into effect immediately.

The 1905 Working Timetable shows 13 up trains and 12 down workings with one return goods service, the latter being worked by an engine. It is probable that increased traffic returns and savings in running costs led to the L & SW relenting in 1907 to the pressure to provide a Sunday service with 7 trains in each direction. The economy of the railmotor can be gleaned from comparison to a conventional motor tank engine of about 3d. and $5\frac{1}{2}$d. per train mile respectively.

NEW WORKS

On 23rd December 1909 a halt was opened at a point close to Durley Mill (at 1 m. 31 ch.) to serve that place and the Calcot and Frogmill areas. This had first been considered in August 1905 but had not been proceeded with. A petition from the inhabitants of Durley for a motor halt received in November evidently prompted the L & SW into action.

Further moves by the residents of Durley were made when a request for a goods siding to be provided near Calcot Bridge was referred to by the L & SW directors on 1st December 1910. Although approved, the company did not undertake the work following refusal by Dr. Maybury to sell the necessary land. Further consideration of a revised plan in 1912 is also believed to have come to nothing when the original estimate of £600 was revised to £900.

FIRST WAR AND AFTER

The outbreak of war had little real impact on the line, with services being maintained throughout the period. Passenger traffic naturally declined owing to the general reluctance to travel. The railmotor cars ceased to operate early on in the hostilities (probably 1915) and conventional locomotives returned. Owing to the pressure upon facilities for treating and convalescing wounded soldiers elsewhere in the county, Northbrook House was temporarily converted into a military hospital. It is believed that from about 1916 some of the injured arrived at Bishop Waltham by rail. Around 1917 the activity increased when some 7,000 troops of the 3rd, 4th, 5th and 6th Battalions of the Hampshire Regiment arrived and were billeted in and around the town, many being accommodated in private domestic dwellings – sometimes as many as five or six per house.

Despite the presence of the military, no special traffic is recalled as having been transported by rail; most required movements of military accoutrements went by road to Gosport or Portsmouth. However, sometime in late 1917 or early 1918 a special troop train was brought up the branch and marshalled ready to take a large number of troops to a camp in Scotland. This must surely have been the heaviest train ever to pass over the line and is recalled as consisting of bogie passenger vehicles hauled by two tender engines. Prior to departure from Bishops Waltham, the train is said to have stretched from the goods shed to beyond the crossing.

Railmotor No. 10 at Bishops Waltham c.1906. Left to right are: Guard George Padwick, Postman Edgar Adams, Porter/Signalman Steve Goulding, Fireman Frank Wills, and Driver Perkins. It was around this time on 18th February 1906 when railmotor No. 8 burst a cylinder on the first down train of the day.   COURTESY JOHN BOSWORTH

Around this time an amusing incident occurred at Bishops Waltham involving a local curate who had disgraced himself in some way and became exceedingly unpopular with the townspeople. On one occasion when he was known to be returning to the town from a visit, a small crowd had gathered at the station to show their disapproval. The staff at Botley being aware of this, hurriedly arranged for the unfortunate curate to travel in a van attached to the train about to depart for Bishops Waltham. Upon arrival at the terminus, the van was detached and moved into the goods shed where the reverend gentleman alighted and was able to avoid the protestations of the assembled group. One economy did take place from 1918 when the timetable shows the Sunday service as having been withdrawn. This was later restored again in 1923 but on a reduced basis with four trains each way instead of seven.

Replacement of the branch telegraph circuit by telephonic communication was authorised on 21st November 1921 at a cost of £46. This may have indirectly been as a result of an incident which had occurred on the 20th June, reported to the Traffic Officers Meeting as follows:

'The Driver of the 3.35 p.m. passenger train from Botley to Bishops Waltham which left Botley at 3.45 p.m. was handed a train tablet which had been brought from Bishops Waltham by the goods train leaving there at 3.25 p.m. without passing the tablet through the instrument at Botley.

'The "train arrival" signal was not given for the Goods train, nor were the necessary bell signals (i.e. the "warning" and "release train tablet" signals used for the 3.35 p.m. passenger train. The "departure" signal for the latter was sent and received at Bishops Waltham. It appears that this signal was understood by the Porter/Signalman at Bishops Waltham to have been sent in error and was not acknowledged.

'There being no telephonic communication between the two stations, the Signalman at Botley could not be questioned and, as the Porter/Signalman at Bishops Waltham did not receive the "call attention" signal, he definitely concluded that the "departure" signal had been wrongly sent and therefore took no steps until at 3.57 p.m. he found that the passenger train was approaching. The irregularity was then reported to the Station Master at Bishops Waltham who subsequently got in touch with the Station Master at Botley on the telegraph instrument when it was arranged that the tablet which had been wrongly dealt with at Botley should be taken back by the 4.30 p.m. passenger train without being passed through the instrument at Bishops Waltham; the indicator of which continued to show "tablet out for up train".

'A joint enquiry held on the 28th June found that the Botley Signalman, when first reporting the irregularity, stated that the tablet brought by the goods train was placed in the instrument and the bookings in his train register record this. In a further report, however, two days later, he admitted that although he had placed the tablet in the slide of the instrument, by an oversight he took it out again without passing it through and clearing the section, and then used it for the passenger train. During the interval between the arrival of the goods train and the departure of the passenger train, his mind was evidently preoccupied with various movements and he forgot to pass the tablet through the instrument. He overlooked the necessity for;

1. giving the "train arrival" signal for the goods train
2. the passing of the tablet through the instrument
3. the giving of the "warning" signal for the passenger train
4. the asking for "tablet release".

'When the passenger train left he seems to have given the "departure" signal as if everything was in order. This train register is an incorrect record. The circumstances point to the fact that the starting signal was not lowered when the 3.35 p.m. passenger train left Botley.

'The Signalman as well as the Driver and Fireman of the train states positively that the starting signal was lowered but the Guard admits that although he saw the tablet handed to the Driver, he did not observe the position of the signal. A testing of the locking later showed it to be in order which indicates the impossibility of the signal being lowered.

'After considering all the circumstances we can only arrive at the conclusion that the Signalman's statement and the statements of the Driver and Fireman regarding the position of the signal is open to much doubt and cannot be accepted.

'The Botley Signalman has been permanently relieved of signal box duties and reduced to the grade of Porter. The train Driver and Guard have been suspended from duty for one day with loss of pay and the Porter/Signalman at Bishops Waltham has been suitably cautioned.'

The area around Botley station, in particular on the east side, was found to be prone to landslips, several occurring in the mid-twenties to mid-thirties period. One such slip happened at 9.40 a.m. on 25th March 1926, blocking the Bishops Waltham line some thirteen yards on the station side of the branch home signal. The effect was also to render the home signal unworkable. The motor train services for the rest of the day, until the 6.15 p.m. departure, terminated on the branch outside of the home signal where passengers had to detrain and walk alongside the line to the down platform.

One of the few recorded derailments on the branch occurred on 25th February 1931, fortunately without any injury. At 3.14 p.m. when the 3.05 p.m. train from Bishops Waltham to Botley, consisting of the usual engine and one coach, was running between Durley Halt and Botley, the leading pair of wheels of the front bogie of the coach became derailed. The driver managed to bring his train to a stand after travelling a distance of 394 yards. The only passenger in the coach was Porter Steve Goulding, who was travelling to Botley to assist in work at that station.

The derailment was caused by the rails spreading when a number of sleeper fastenings gave way, allowing the nearside wheel of the coach to drop off the rail and the offside wheel to climb over the outside rail of the curve. An examination later revealed the sleepers at this point to be rotten despite having been laid in 1921. The remaining day's timetable had to be cancelled and passengers conveyed by road. Rerailment of the offending coach was effected at 6.55 p.m. by the Eastleigh breakdown train which had arrived on the scene at 4.15 p.m. The line was re-opened by the first train the following morning with a 20 m.p.h. speed limit in force.

DECLINE AND FALL

The incident described above with the 3.05 p.m. train from Bishops Waltham, without a single revenue-paying passenger on board, perhaps illustrates the situation of falling passenger receipts. Its zenith now passed, economy was to be the order of the day.

With effect from 1st February 1931 the Sunday service was withdrawn for the third and final time in the line's history. The Southern Railway, who had assumed responsibilities at the Grouping in 1923, stated that 42 train miles per week would be saved. As a result of this and other similar economies elsewhere, a saving in wages of £375 per annum would be affected. Arrangements were made with the local carrier to

Alec Summerville and his family on an outing during the final years of the passenger service on the branch. The return fare to Botley was 3½d at this time. A Mr. Bullock, who lived in the town, was a solicitor's clerk in London and commuted to Waterloo daily on the 8 a.m. train to Botley.
CTY. JOHN BOSWORTH

deliver the milk churns (left at Bishops Waltham by farmers) to Wickham for forwarding on.

On 14th July the system of tablet working was replaced by train staff and 'one engine in steam' operation. The staff had a key on one end which unlocked the ground frame controlling Edwards' siding just south of Bishops Waltham.

By 1931 the weekday passenger train service had reduced to six in each direction with one down working denoted as 'mixed' (see timetable in Appendix 8). A comparison with the 1927 timetable (also reproduced) reveals the evening services as being the main victims of the economy measures, no doubt to save on staff overtime.

Inevitably this pruning was only a portent of what was to follow and on 10th October 1932 the SR reported that:

'In consequence of falling passenger traffic the passenger service on the Bishops Waltham line should be withdrawn after Saturday 31st December, and the 23 season ticket holders have been given notice accordingly.
The following economies will be made:–

1. Saving of branch engine and two sets of enginemen
   – immediate economy, coal, oil, etc.   £420
   – two sets of enginemen, when absorbed   £800
   – withdrawal of one clerk and one porter from Bishops
     Waltham   £313
                                                                 ──────
                                                                 £1,533

2. Less estimated cost of road conveyance by
   the Company's delivery agent of fish,
   and other parcels traffic @ 30/– per week   £78
                                                                 ──────
                                 Net economy   £1,455

'The estimated value of the passenger and season ticket traffic on the branch for a year is £755 of which £570 represents contributory value.
'The effect on the mileage will be a saving of 222 passenger train miles and 87 mixed train miles per week.'

In the days long before the closure of a railway brought the local populace and enthusiasts flocking in for some sort of celebration, the last day of passenger services on the Bishops Waltham line attracted little attention, the whole affair being somewhat mute. However, fortunately, the reporter for the *Hampshire Observer* recorded the event in lyrical fashion and, although displaying an historical naivety, she nevertheless leaves us with an affectionate portrait reproduced in full below:

'Closing Incidents on the Botley–Bishops Waltham Line

On December 31st 1932 the short length of single railway track which connects Botley with Bishops Waltham was closed to passenger traffic. The service has had such an extended decline that the final passing was almost unnoticed as virtually the line has been a dying concern for years. Although there was little outward manifestation of the suspension of the rail service, those of the public who used the train and others who have been accustomed to see it puffing across country every day have not parted with it without some pangs of regret as what has become an integral part of their daily calling. It would appear that the little train had not only served the convenience of the travelling public, but like the sun, has served to mark the hours of the passing day for as one well known market gardener and fruit grower who works beside the railway track has put it "how on earth am I to know the time when the Bishops Waltham train stops running?"

'I decided to make the last trip from Botley to Bishops Waltham and vice versa on Saturday and was rather surprised to find that the public had not embraced the opportunity to "make history". As a matter of fact when we left Botley station promptly to time on Saturday evening the only passengers on board were the Stationmaster Mr. H. Wright, Messrs. W. H. Smith & Son's bookstall attendant and myself. The train was in the charge of Driver Frank Wills of Eastleigh and Fireman William Firth of Eastleigh. I was particularly struck with the twisting nature of the route and learned from the Driver that in the short $3\frac{3}{4}$ miles of track there were three complete S bends whilst there were 8,850 sleepers in actual use. The little engine is easily capable of a speed of round about 35 m.p.h. but the actual running time is limited to 25 m.p.h.

'On the return journey from Bishops Waltham a little more interest was shown in the departure of the last train and a few more adventurous spirits joined the train to be numbered among the really last passengers to cover the journey. Here I saw Mr. Thomas Cuell who for over 43 years has operated the signals and level

Class D1 0—4—2T No. B240 leaving Botley on the last day of passenger services over the branch. The Eastleigh-based ex-LB & SCR tanks shared duties with Class O2s in the final years with A12 0—4—2s and the occasional 0395 or 700 class engines on goods services.

HAMPSHIRE TELEGRAPH & POST AND SOUTHERN DAILY ECHO

crossing gates at Bishops Waltham station and had the distinction of signalling out the last train and closing the line to passenger traffic. One perchanced and quite unexpected little incident almost passed unnoticed as a lady standing on the station platform squeezed into the hands of Driver Wills a handsome silver cigarette case filled with cigarettes as a farewell gift.

'The older generation who remember the actual laying of the track 68 years ago have practically all passed away but there seems reasonable grounds for the belief that the railway line was laid by a private syndicate for use as a passenger line and in its early days proved of very useful service to the flourishing brickyard and clay works owned by Mr. Mark Blanchard. It was not until some years afterwards that the LSW Railway Company acquired the line. Many people often express surprise that the line runs only from Botley to Bishops Waltham and ends in a cul-de-sac but tradition has it that the original intention was that the line should be extended into the rich agricultural villages in the Meon Valley. This scheme however never matured. But this much is certain that the country between Bishops Waltham and Brockbridge was surveyed with a view to the exploration of the possibilities of an extension of the railway line but for some reason or other nothing tangible was the result. There seems to be no doubt that in bygone days Bishops Waltham was a flourishing market town and the shopping centre for a very wide country district, but the opening of the railway line through the Meon Valley between Fareham and Alton coupled with the coming of the motor car and a network of road motor buses has robbed the old town of much of its former prosperity.

'It is interesting to recall that 23 years ago (23rd January 1910) the Railway Company decided to make a halt for passengers at Durley level crossing, and the passengers who made use of this stopping place will miss the train as much as anyone as there is no bus service from the Calcot or Frogmill areas. Driver Wills drove the first train to make the halt and also the last train to close it again.

'Before Durley level crossing was raised to the dignity of a platform and a shelter for passengers, the old level crossing keeper, the late Mr. Harry Elliott, used to come out on the approach of a train and wave a green light to indicate to the Driver that all was clear. Mr. Elliott also helped to lay the first metals. The first passenger to travel from Bishops Waltham to Durley Halt was the late Mr. Oliver Daggrell of Bishops Waltham and the last passengers to join the train from Durley Halt to Botley on Saturday were Mrs. Tubbs, the level crossing keeper, and her daughter Miss Winnie Tubbs.

'The Botley–Bishops Waltham line has passed through many vicissitudes and originally had a resident Stationmaster who was in charge also of Botley station. Later the two stations were placed under separate control and remained so until the recent retirement of Mr. S. Blount, when the two stations came under the control of Mr. H. W. Jones who resides at Botley station.

'In former days a full set train made frequent journeys between Botley and Bishops Waltham for 12 hours each day with a regular Sunday service but in recent times a self-contained rail coach has been in use and has provided ample accommodation for the needs of the branch. In recent years about fifteen schoolchildren and a handful of season ticket holders have been the mainstay of the line. There has been a constant paring down of the staff and some years ago the guard was entirely dispersed with. The future of the remaining staff is uncertain, but as the line will still be kept open

for heavy merchandise and miscellaneous traffic a skeleton staff will at least remain.

'The little train has for many years pursued the "even tenor of its way" disturbed only by an occasional derailment or a failure of the electric tablet apparatus but the line really came into the news a few years ago when a steer from a neighbouring farm broke loose and stubbornly refused to leave the line with the result that the train had to proceed in a series of spurts and jolts as the steer

Botley station staff gather for the final trip to Waltham. Left to right: Fireman William Firth, Driver Frank Wills, F. Iremonger, Station Master Herbert Wright-Jones and Porters J. Stubbing and H. Carpenter.   SOUTHERN DAILY ECHO

leisurely made its way along the railway track and eventually ended up in a garden at Botley where it was shot.

'It is significant that a day or so ago a collector of old railway tickets made a special journey to Botley to try to secure one of the last series of tickets to be issued to passengers on this branch line. In a farewell conversation with Driver Wills he naturally fell into reminiscent mood and recalled his associations for over 23 years ago with former servants of the Company, mentioning the late Guard George Padwick and Relief Guard Steve Goulding whilst he paid eloquent tribute to the courtesy and kindness of the travelling public with whom he had come into contact and to whom incidentally I formed the opinion he had given the utmost civility in return. He was almost fond in his praise of the twelve different Firemen who had shared the footplate of his engine, and the goodwill which had always existed between him and his mates. I also met Mr. Harry Carpenter, Foreman of the uniform staff at Botley who for 41 successive years has been associated with the working of the railway's line.

Perhaps the brightest and certainly the most lively passengers of the train have been the schoolchildren and it was a very kindly thought on the part of the schoolgirls which prompted them on their last trip before the Christmas holidays to present Driver Wills with a box of cigars, a box of cigarettes and a necktie, each of them receiving in return a dainty little silk handkerchief as a simple token of remembrance from Driver Wills who was deservedly a favourite with the girls.   V.C.'

Hampshire Observer
7th January 1933

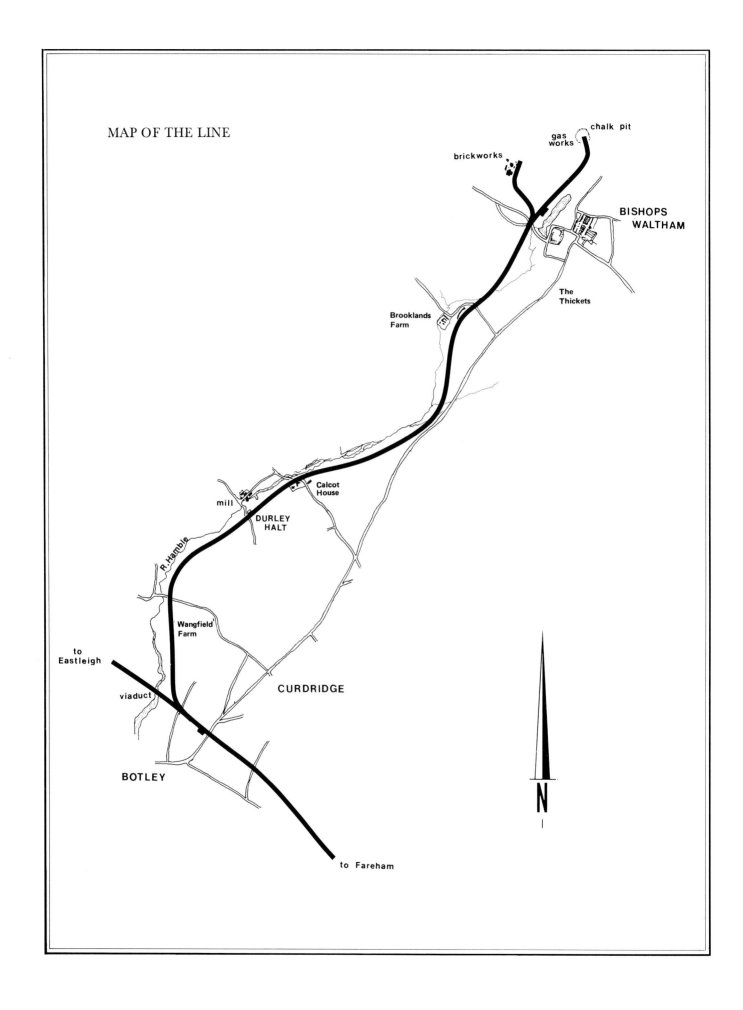

MAP OF THE LINE

chalk pit

gas works

brickworks

BISHOPS WALTHAM

The Thickets

Brooklands Farm

mill

Calcot House

DURLEY HALT

R. Hamble

Wangfield Farm

to Eastleigh

viaduct

CURDRIDGE

BOTLEY

to Fareham

N

CHAPTER FOUR

THE LINE DESCRIBED
A RURAL RIDE

Class O2 0–4–4T awaiting departure time from Botley on 7th November 1928. The rather grand station nameboard, as seen on page 57, has been replaced by one of the ubiquitous Southern Railway concrete versions so manifest around the system in replacement programmes at this time. The oil lamps remain, giving rise to the local residents' nickname of 'Paraffin Junction'. H. C. CASSERLEY

TAKING the summer working timetable for 1927, the first departure of the day was the 7.50 a.m. passenger train from Bishops Waltham. Upon arrival at Botley the engine, usually an '02' class 0–4–4T, would run around its train and back down past the signal box to couple onto the opposite end of the single coach ready for the return journey. A twenty minute stop-over allowed activities to take place at a leisurely pace, time for the engine crew to exchange a word with the guard whilst the few passengers for the 8.20 a.m. made their way across the footbridge without undue haste.

Branch trains started from the bay behind the down platform, enabling Bishops Waltham services independent access to the station. When the guard indicated 'right away', the single coach train pulled slowly out of the platform past the signal box where the fireman picked up the train tablet before the loco gathered speed curving away from the main line, passing under the separate arch of the bridge shared with the route to Eastleigh.

A northerly direction was assumed on a descent of 1 in 100 as the course entered the Valley of the Hamble River on a low embankment, the main line to Eastleigh disappearing to the left over the six-arch viaduct spanning the river. After passing through a wooded area, the first of several occupation crossings was encountered serving the Wangfield Estate which the railway skirted to reach the first underbridge bisecting Wang-

Taken from a passing train, the branch can be seen curving away from the Eastleigh–Fareham line. The water pipe carried over the line at this point was fixed to the bridge and had been the subject of some correspondence between Sir Henry Jenkyns and the LSWR in 1894. A. E. BENNETT

The first of two girder underbridges at Wangfield Lane. The slight structure of these gave credence to the mistaken view prevailing at one time that the branch was a 'light' railway. The white railings are a later feature added sometime between 1930 and 1950. Around 1905 two children decided to attempt to stop a train at the bridge by piling up faggots on the running line. Their misguided efforts were successful but they were caught and birched for their trouble.   AUTHOR

field Lane, about half a mile from Botley. This simple yet graceful girder structure took the line over the road from Calcot village. Close by is Wangfield House, once the seat of William Godwin, and described in an 1859 guide as a 'neat mansion in the Elizabethan style'.

Swinging north-eastward, the route followed the natural course of the Hamble on a brief descent of 1 in 198, followed by a steady climb of 1 in 114 to the public level crossing at Durley Mill. Small plantations dividing stretches of open farmland interrupt the view of the river to the left, meandering its course to the Hamble estuary some seven miles distant. Far from intruding, the railway here blends naturally with the rural environment, with no major earthworks or structures to blemish the landscape.

Passing the cluster of small cottages forming the hamlet of Frogmill (built around the mill itself originally for the mill workers) the driver shuts off steam and the single engine and carriage drift over the occupation crossing, brakes were applied and a brief whistle sounded to herald the train's approach to the cinder platform forming the tiny Halt at Durley. With no passengers alighting, often the only person to greet the train at the end of the platform was Alice Tubb, the crossing keeper, who exchanged a few words with the guard as the morning papers were handed out along with a parcel or two destined for the Mill cottages.

With a slight jolt the train was off again, over the level crossing and on up the barely apparent 1 in 580 gradient with surprising stealth, the gentle exhaust nevertheless disturbing the tranquility of the surrounding country. The line was fairly straight at this point as the train approached Calcot bridge, the second underbridge which shared the same graceful girders

Sadly, this damaged photograph is the only known view of Durley Halt. The wooden shelter was a slightly later addition provided just under a year from the opening of the station in December 1909. Workers at nearby Durley Mill were probably almost the only source of passenger traffic as the village was some distance away and in later years it was more convenient to catch the bus into Bishops Waltham (a bus service was started by the Crabb Brothers around 1925). Perhaps it was for this reason that in a competition run by a railway magazine, Durley once won the unenviable title of the station in Britain one was most unlikely to alight at! No goods traffic was handled here except small parcels and the morning papers which were tossed out from the first up train. The crossing keeper's cottage had existed some years before the Halt was erected.   COLLECTION MALCOLM SNELLGROVE

A rare glimpse of a railmotor on the branch c.1909 at Calcot Bridge. Proposals in 1910 and 1912 for a siding close by to serve Durley Mill were not carried out; traffic was always dealt with at Botley, transported by horse and cart from the mill.

COURTESY JACK TICKNER

An 1899 view of the 'Waltham Jack' passing the Thickets just south of Bishops Waltham, hauled by an unidentified O2 class 0—4—4T.
Just out of view to the left was Edwards Siding by the occupation crossing to Brooklands Farm. This held about 5-6 wagons but was out
of use by 1932.
COURTESY JOHN BOSWORTH

as the first. Here the public road was lowered by about four feet when the railway was under construction, to allow a 15 ft clearance for road traffic, the lightly constructed girder sections providing for a 20 feet width between the brick supporting walls. Near this point on the right was Calcot House, the residence for many years of the Jenkyns family, local land-owners and benefactors to both Curdridge and Botley.

A little further on, two miles from Botley, another wood was bisected by the line's passage, and beyond, as the view opened out on both sides of the line, the train entered a shallow cutting, eventually passing over a shallow stream. Looking eastwards from here was the first view of the Botley to Bishops Waltham road, generally taking a more southerly route serving the village of Curdridge. The close proximity of road and railway was brief as the line turned northward crossing a tributary of the Hamble river followed by the course of an old Roman road. Open farmland was particularly apparent at this point as the railway followed the natural contours of the landscape on the gentlest of embankments.

As the train approached Brooklands Farm occupation cross-ing, the engine whistle was heard, followed by the sudden clatter as it passed over the points leading to the private siding of Messrs. Edwards' Brewers from the Abbey Brewery whose traffic had been dealt with here from around 1900. From here

the gentle ascent increased from 1 in 200 to 1 in 100 for the final approach to the terminus some half-mile distant and the final bridge carried the line over the upper reaches of the infant Hamble.

Then just ahead could be seen the southern approach of Bishops Waltham. As the train entered the last short cutting, the driver eased the regulator and gently slowed with the level crossing in view. To the east were the Palace ruins and the Abbey Mill, both notable landmarks of the town and as the train brakes were applied, upon looking out of the window of the carriage, the figure of Thomas Cuell, the Bishops Waltham signalman, could be seen outside the box waiting to collect the train tablet pouch. A smooth 'catch' was made in the effortless ritual as the fireman surrendered the tablet and the train clattered over the level crossing, drawing up sharply at the platform.

Passengers alighting from the train were confronted with the first view of the imposing station house, large by any standard for a line of this nature, a lasting legacy of the dreams of the directors of the original BWR Company. Closer inspection would reveal the beautiful and unique terracotta work, an advertisement and testimony of the products from the nearby brickworks. While the coal merchants were busy shovelling coal from one of a pair of colliery wagons opposite the platform,

The approach to the terminus c.1910. The fields in the foreground were the scene of regular cattle sales which generated 'tail' traffic for the branch. Occasionally this necessitated special trains of cattle and sheep with accommodation vehicles for the dealers and farmers who had come from long distances.
AUTHORS' COLLECTION

the engine would run round its coach and a few passengers might arrive for the return departure at 8.50 a.m.

This was the start of a typical day on the branch in the years following the Great War. The short journey was quite uneventful and the route, with its easy gradients and earthworks, was more akin to a light railway. The 1927 service timetable shows nine weekday passenger workings with an extra midday train on Saturdays. The 10.55 a.m. departure from Botley is interesting as this is shown as a mixed working. Returning goods vehicles were conveyed in a separate goods train leaving Bishops Waltham at 6.30 p.m., the engine on completion of shunting movements at Botley returning light to Bishops Waltham to work the 7.15 p.m. passenger service. The normal travelling time allowed on the branch was 10 minutes for passenger workings, but the mixed train referred to was diagrammed 15 minutes, suggesting an allowance for shunting at Edwards' siding.

On Sundays four trains in each direction were provided, the solitary morning train, leaving Botley at 8.10 a.m. and returning at 8.44 a.m., being a through service from Eastleigh. This working by an Eastleigh engine and crew avoided the need for the local engineman to come on duty to prepare their engine until the next departure, the 5.15 p.m. train from Bishops Waltham. Three return trips were made in this early evening period, the last arriving at Bishops Waltham at 8.10 p.m., allowing the engine crew to book off at around 8.30 p.m.

In 'goods only' days, taking at random the arrangements pertaining to 1955, the service commenced from Eastleigh as an independent working, arriving at Botley around 9.15 a.m. usually in the charge of 'M7' class No. 30376. After shunting the yard, vehicles destined for Bishops Waltham would form the 9.40 a.m. train up the branch. At this time the train consisted of around 3 to 6 wagons, mainly coal, mill traffic and building materials, with a considerable number of parcels brought about by the large post-war growth in general mail order catalogue methods of trading. The journey at this time was notable for the weeds growing through the track and the slapping of leaves and branches against the sides of the train as the undergrowth sought to take over a route where maintenance was kept to a bare minimum.

Upon arrival at Bishops Waltham, the coal wagons would be shunted into the back siding for the coal merchant, wagons containing mill traffic for Messrs Dukes were left on the goods shed siding, whilst vans and other traffic were dealt with direct from the main platform. A sixty minute stop-over was allowed for shunting requirements, the return working departing at 11.00 a.m. The train guard acting as shunter for the trip, was also responsible for opening and closing the gates at Durley crossing. At Botley the engine would work its train across to the yard and undertake shunting duties as required before working back to Eastleigh.

The terminus as seen from Victoria Road about 1909. On the extreme right is part of the rear of the signalbox. The window, just visible, was provided in 1907 for sighting road traffic more easily.
LENS OF SUTTON

THE STATIONS

BISHOPS WALTHAM

The approach from the east. Entry to the station was gained by the road off to the right which also served the yard and goods shed. An 1862 proposal to replace the planned level crossing by an underbridge was not carried out owing to the expense which would also have involved draining part of the pond.
AUTHORS' COLLECTION

The coming of the railway to Bishops Waltham considerably enhanced the town's claim as the shopping centre and flourishing focal point for a very wide country district. In truth markets held here from about the thirteenth century had all but ceased by 1841 owing to the development of Botley following the opening of the Gosport branch of the London & Southampton Railway. It was not until the early 1860s when the various schemes promoted by Sir Arthur Helps leading to the opening of the Clay Works, Gas Works, Water Works and an Infirmary* came to fruition and the all important opening of the railway in 1863, that Bishops Waltham could be regarded as a business centre in addition to its traditional roles in agriculture and milling.

This was reflected in the traffic dealt with at Bishops Waltham, the considerable goods and merchandise over the years contrasting with the lack of growth in passenger business.

The first traders in the town to use the railway were naturally the Clay Company which received supplies of coal and coke and were able to ship bricks, tiles and other terracotta material to a wider market. Bishops Waltham Gas Works received coal from both Brays Down Coal Company and Somersetshire Coal Company and timber from Messrs. Gamblin's Sawmills at Newtown. Coal merchants handling the town's supplies at first were Messrs. Geo. & Edwd. Clark, who also traded as grocers, drapers, millers and maltsters, and William Cooper who also received timber traffic. By 1890 Messrs. Reeves and Tebbutt had taken a wharf at the station and later The Colliery Supply

Co. had a wharf from about 1910. Other coal merchants trading at this time were Messrs. Jas. August Sanger of Newtown, Messrs. King & Privett, and William Hatchett of Station Road. The latter is known to have had his own wagons, believed to have been painted brown with white lettering. Mr. Myers of Swanmore also received coal and other goods which were carted by road from Bishops Waltham.

A considerable traffic in farm produce was dealt with from the early days, despite the recession of the period, the station becoming the railhead for the numerous farms scattered around the lower Meon Valley, a situation enjoyed until the line's closure in 1962.

Most of the produce handled was arable, mainly cereal crops, wheat, barley, oats etc. but there were regular movements of tail traffic, especially at the times of the cattle and sheep sales when as many as 600 to 700 animals could be dealt with, often in complete train formations. Horse movements were also prevalent, reaching an annual peak at the time of the Hambledon races, which were run at Grenville Hall. During the hunting season riders and their mounts also arrived to join the meets of the Hambledon hounds. Milk sent out daily originated from several farms including Mr. Greenwood, Mr. Trigg and Edwards (Tangier Farm) and was usually of the order of just five or six churns. One farmer, Charlie West, is remembered for bringing his churns to the station using a mule and dray and usually being late. The station would look out for him and hold the train up until he arrived.

The fruit growing season yielded mainly soft fruit packed in baskets tied around with a bandage and loaded into the

---

* The Infirmary was never used for its original purpose.

29

Bishops Waltham signal box would appear to date from 1885 as an LSWR directors' minute of 4th March that year reports that inter-locking of points and signals was either incomplete or wanting altogether and that the branch was not worked under the 'electric block system'. Further to these 'improvements' being carried out, the design of the box was a standard one of the 1884-8 period found in considerable numbers in the Bournemouth area. The frame was probably Stevens and had 16 levers with 2 spare. A later postcard view of the rear of the building shows a window added in the back of the box, evidently for the signalman to view traffic approaching the crossing. The steps on the south end of the box were replaced or repositioned against the side wall and at the same time the landing was enclosed with a porch. Although no official record of these alterations has been discovered, they probably date from about 1911. The box was open between 7.15 a.m. and 9.15 p.m. daily and in this view the station complement of porter/signalmen are present, along with postman Edgar Adams. As early as 1926 the working of the line by electric tablet was questioned by the SR administration at Waterloo. Following a review of working by the District Superintendent's office, it was felt justified to continue tablet working owing to the large traffic requirements of the May and October cattle sales which generated up to 70 separate loads of cattle over both days. However, this economy was eventually made on 6th July 1931 when 'one engine in steam' working was introduced. The signal box was eventually closed in December 1935 when the signals were removed and the points operated by local hand levers.
COURTESY JOHN BOSWORTH

Looking up to the Winchester Road c.1910. The building in the centre of the view is the coal merchants' office, at this time occupied by the Colliery Supply Company. It was later taken over by Messrs. J. E. Smith of Portsmouth who were associated with the line until closure. The other coal merchants based here did not have offices but leased wharfage at the far end of the line.

COURTESY JOHN BOSWORTH

respective wagon with greaseproof paper in between. Other seasonal traffic included the inward movement of fish and crabs from the Hamble Estuary. These were packed between ice in wicker hampers or fish straps which were sent down from Hull or Grimsby. Around 1912 the price for a whole cod was about two shillings.

The local brewing and milling industries in the town were served with regular deliveries of wheat and other cereal crops to the Abbey Mill and outward movement of grain sugar beet, animal feedstuffs, fertilizers and hops and sugar for Edwards Brewery. The first miller to use the line was probably John Hague who was trading at the Abbey Mill around 1867. Later by 1890, the business was operated by Henry Frank Hurley who were also brewers and wine & spirit merchants, running this side of the business at the Abbey Brewery. From 1902, following several changes of occupants, the Abbey Mill was taken over by Messrs. James Duke & Son who began a long association with the town which still continues the milling trade to this day.

Messrs. James Duke & Son generated a considerable volume of traffic over the years, mainly oats, barley, wheat and maize. These products were received in quantities of around 100 tons per delivery, loaded in sacks, usually requiring five to six wagons. A large proportion of this produce originated from as far afield as Argentina. It arrived in barges at Nine Elms where it was transhipped for onward transit by rail. Fertilizers received from Avonmouth and London were carted by road direct to farms. Large consignments of seed potatoes were also received when in season. Outward traffic included oats and grain bound for most southern counties and occasionally as far as the Channel Islands.

Duke's traffic was handled on the goods shed siding by their own employees. Despite some seasonal increases, rail traffic was constant throughout the calendar. Most seasonal goods balanced each other, and only declined in the late 1950s when the firm's policy was changed to road transport. An analysis of surviving ledgers shows that annual cartage charges paid to the LSWR in the period around the First War averaged £460, increasing by the mid 1920s to around £1,640. Unfortunately traffic volumes are not recorded.

Other general traffic dealt with included large quantities of sugar beet from local farms each October. This crop was controlled under a permit system whereby farmers were contracted to grow predetermined quantities on a quota basis. The outgoing loads, about 3–4 wagons a day, were sent mainly to King's Lynn, Cambridge and Kidderminster. A notable quantity of manure traffic was also dealt with and this came from as far afield as Yorkshire. By the mid 1930s the seasonal soft fruit produce had ceased as the relatively small number of growers found competition from the large market gardeners to Botley and the south too fierce.

Around the turn of the century Messrs. Edward & Sons, operating from the Abbey Brewery, entered into a working agreement for a 55 yard private siding situated on the west side of the line about $\frac{1}{2}$ mile south of the station. In 'goods only' days the siding was controlled by a ground frame unlocked by the train staff. Hops, malt and other goods used in the trade were received and transported to the brewery in hand carts. No outward traffic was dealt with here. It was also used for farm traffic as required, particularly nearby Brooklands Farm. Its use declined in the immediate post-war years and it was eventually removed around September 1948.

Bishops Waltham station around 1906. The station canopy date from at least 1895. The wooden side screens to the station canopy date from at least 1895. The wooden box mounted on the nearest screen housed a fire hose which, along with others provided, was checked monthly. Station staff at this time consisted of the station master (class 4), two porter/signalmen, one booking clerk, one goods clerk (checker), one porter/guard and one passenger guard.

AUTHORS' COLLECTION

Railmotor No. 1 at Bishops Waltham in November 1904 shortly after introduction on the branch. The gate in the fence just in front of of the train was the main entry to the station platform. Interesting features in this view are the coal merchants' weighing scales and the wire stays from the station house supporting the canopy.

Two other private sidings (apart from the one described on page 10) were also provided in the station area, both dating from the earliest years of the railway. One of these originally served the chalk and lime workings of the Bishops Waltham Clay Company and was in effect a northwards continuation of the running line from the goods yard. Part of this siding was taken over by the Bishops Waltham Gas & Coke Company upon the opening of their works in March 1864. Here coal wagons would be received and manhandled into position for unloading to the retorts. Outgoing traffic consisted of coke and tar. By 1922, arrangements had been made for other firms to deal with wagon loads on this siding. The minute books record the LSWR entering into a working agreement in December with Messrs. Thos. Pink, builder; Messrs. Hewitt & Hill, timber merchants; The Shell Mex Co. and the Gas Company. The siding was described as being 'of very old standing' and would be worked as follows:

'The traffic for the siding is placed by the LSW Co. at the boundary gate and outgoing wagons are accepted at that point. The rates for traffic include terminals and it is not considered advisable to provide for the payment of any shunting charge.'

The private siding laid to serve the Clay Company's Works was almost certainly in use from the opening of the BWR. The works were later taken over by M. H. Blanchard & Co and the history and development of the brickworks are described in Appendix 1. Blanchards received around one or two wagons of coal each day when the works were in full production, and the despatch of bricks, tiles and other terracotta material often amounted to some three to four wagons a day. A revision to the siding agreement between the L&SW and Messrs. Blanchards made in 1917 refers to the present arrangement whereby 'traffic is worked over the siding by their own private engine' but no more details are known. The Agreement prescribed that the LSWR would work wagons only to and from the boundary gate. On 12th June 1901 the L&SW agreed to provide an additional siding to deal with Blanchards' brick traffic at an estimated cost of £253. The agreement was extended from 19th December 1917 to include the reception of traffic for Mr. E. W. Hewett, an auctioneer who wished to handle goods to and from auction sales. The agreement was to include a payment of 2/– per wagon over and above the normal Bishops Waltham rates in respect of each loaded wagon.

The ownership of the siding changed hands when the brickworks were taken over by Messrs. Elliott Bros. in 1918. Although the siding agreement with the L&SW continued unchanged, an amendment was eventually made in December 1924 between Elliotts and the newly formed Southern Railway to the effect that Elliotts were to maintain the portion of the siding on their property and the SR were to deliver traffic to a point close to the works but to receive wagons at the boundary point with Elliotts. The station rates applied to traffic plus a special haulage charge of 1/6d per wagon. Inevitably with minimal maintenance, the siding is recalled falling into poor condition, doubtless aggravated by the marshy area near Pondside Lane (sometimes referred to as Sawmill Lane) which was prone to flooding when the water table rose.

A 1914 photograph, looking towards Botley. Comparison with the previous view reveals some alterations to the canopy roof which appear to have eliminated the need for the stays. The horse-chestnut tree on the extreme left was a distinctive feature which survived until the final years. The station was gas-lit from the earliest days, the supply being the subject of much correspondence in the 1880s between the LSWR and the Bishops Waltham Gas and Coke Company over charges.   COURTESY JOHN BOSWORTH

The following is an extract from the SR 1934 working time-table Appendix:

BISHOPS WALTHAM BRANCH

Clay Works siding. – The siding terminates in a loop at the Clay Works, the points leading to this loop being situated about 370 yards from the Company's boundary.

The siding is under the control of the Station Master at Botley, and no traffic must be worked to or from the siding except under his direction.

Wagons containing traffic consigned to Messrs. Elliott Bros. will be placed by the Company's engine at a spot on the Bishops Waltham side of the points leading to the loop at the Clay Works, and the Company's engine must not pass beyond that point. Wagons containing traffic from Messrs. Elliott Bros. will be worked by them to the boundary point.

Before wagons are worked to the Clay Works siding, the Station Master at Botley must arrange with Messrs. Elliott Bros. for the boundary gate to be opened and secured for movements into and out of the siding, and for the siding to be kept clear.

The catch points are operated by a level on the ground, and the man in charge of the movements in and out of the siding will be held responsible for seeing that these points are in the correct position for movements over same.

The portion of the siding between the Company's boundary and the entrance to the loop adjacent to the Clay Works may be used for the Railway Company's own purposes.

Despite the healthy goods receipts, passenger traffic always remained light, with only schoolchildren and a few regular travellers to Botley and Southampton the mainstay of the service. One regular traveller, conspicuous in this quiet situation, was a Mr. Bullock, a London solicitor, who commuted to Waterloo daily during the 1920s. In the years before the spread of the motor car, commercial travellers often used the line to reach the town, many staying at the Crown Hotel overnight.

Around the period of the First War the occasional special excursion was run, one annual event recalled being the local Sunday School outing to Lee-on-the-Solent. During the high season, weekday excursion tickets were available to Portsmouth, Bournemouth and other South coast resorts from time to time, but the outbreak of war marked an end to these treats, and the general reluctance of people to travel during this period was probably a key factor in the withdrawal of the Sunday service:

Parcels were collected for delivery to the shops each day by the Crown Hotel who for many years were agents for Suttons of Reading. The proprietors were a Miss Williams and Mrs. Bond. Regular deliveries are recalled as including small machine tools, drugs and carboys of distilled water for the chemist. Mail was picked up daily from the station, in the early days by hand cart in the charge of Toby Tilbury and others. Around 1920 this was usually two full sacks each day. Later a Mr. Stubbs operated with a horse and cart delivering mails as far as Botley when the station was closed. Parcels traffic increased steadily over the years as the mail order system of trading by organisations such as Empire Stores and Littlewoods became popular. Deliveries thus became destined for individuals rather than the shops. An interesting regular traffic over the line was the transfer of surplus coinage from Lloyds Bank in the town to their larger Southampton offices. This occurred about once a month when the coinage, sealed and padlocked in one or more metal-bound boxes, was collected by the local carrier in mid-afternoon and taken to the station to be sent out by an early evening train to Botley.

The first carriers at the station were probably Henry Lomer and Peter Emmett who are known to have been operating from 1875 to at least 1895. They were later replaced by Arthur Paskins. A list of appointed carriers along with station masters at both Bishops Waltham and Botley appears in Appendix 7.

A rationalisation of the taxi service operating from the station appears to have occurred in the early 1920s when Mr. King relinquished his horse cab privilege. Two years later, on 29th December, Mr. Robinson also withdrew his cab service. Mr. King was a partner of King & Privett, the coal merchants and carriers who had taken the public and carrier licence from the Crown Hotel some years before. The carrier side of the business was continued, however, through the firm's existence.

By the 1930s, the coal merchants receiving deliveries in the yard were Messrs. J. E. Smith, the aforementioned King & Privett, M. J. Davies and Hulme. The last three firms operated with two lorries each, King & Privett's being 1 ton model T Ford vehicles. Their coal pens were located in front of the goods shed, but there was no office at the station as the firm worked from their home base in the town. King & Privett obtained their coal from collieries in Yorkshire (soft coal), Nottingham (Bakers Nuts), and Wales (anthracite). Coke was supplied from gas works in Portsmouth. They did not have their own wagons, but hired them from Messrs. J. R. Woods of Southampton. These vehicles were painted orange with black lettering and carried small plates marked 'return to Bishops Waltham'. Deliveries amounted to about 25 to 30 tons per week until the early 1940s when the firm ceased the coal side of the business and concentrated on the carrier service, using a 3 ton Austin lorry. Messrs. Hulme also operated a carrier service but covered the area to the west of Bishops

A poor quality but rare view taken by an intrepid employee of Messrs. Dukes who mounted the roof of the Abbey Mill to snap this 1920s shot of the station area. The siding leading to Blanchard's brickworks can clearly be seen in the centre of the photograph with the small level crossing over Sawmill Lane at the extreme top. In the top right is one of the few glimpses of the engine shed which could hold two tank engines (with smokeboxes facing out). It was equipped with an 18in parallel jaw vice, a sand furnace, a selection of spanners, oil cans, lamps, cotton waste and a pit between the running line which flooded every time an exceptionally high tide came up the River Hamble from Southampton water!
COURTESY JOHN BOSWORTH

Messrs. J. E. Smith's yard and lorry, taken on the last day of the passenger service. Smith's coal wagon is lettered with the firm's main bases in the East Hampshire area including Bishops Waltham.   HAMPSHIRE TELEGRAPH & POST

The back siding used by Messrs. J. E. Smith for coal deliveries. The various types of coal can clearly be seen. Inward deliveries of coal to the various merchants based here averaged about twelve wagons per day in 1929.   REV. DAVID LITTLEFAIR

The approach and station forecourt in the final years of the passenger service. The width of the area in front of the station building was restricted by the pond. It appears the area was 'tarpaved' in October 1898 by Droxford District Council, the LSWR contributing £15 towards the total cost. From 1927 passenger receipts were in steep decline, by 1929 the daily average number of tickets issued at Bishops Waltham was twenty-five with about twenty-five season ticket holders. The average number of passengers per train was five and only rarely was a total of twenty exceeded. Closure had been considered in October 1930 but this was deferred by the SR Board until 1932. Interestingly, by 1930 passenger trains were being worked without a guard. COURTESY JOHN BOSWORTH

Waltham around their base in Upham, most of the goods conveyed by these firms at this time consisting of 'smalls', parcels and personal luggage forwarded in advance. It is interesting that whereas neither carrier generally visited Botley, Messrs. Hill, the firm based there, did make regular deliveries to Bishops Waltham. Presumably Botley was generally only seen as a forwarding point whereas Bishops Waltham was a destination in its own right.

Messrs. J. E. Smith, who had a well established coal business in Portsmouth, took a wharf at the station in 1921. This was located opposite the station buildings and served by a siding trailing into the brickworks siding. Soon after the brickworks siding was removed in 1947 the siding was extended further south and the wharf and office were moved to a point hard by the level crossing. The annual tonnage handled, originally around 2,000 tons, later increased to between 3,000 to 4,000 tons around the period of the Second War. During the 1950s, however, this declined to about 1,000 to 1,500 tons. Following the closure of the branch in 1962, the firm had to cart their coal products from their wharf at Botley station.

Supplies were obtained primarily from Blackwell Colliery (who supplied their best grade) and also Sedling (Nottingham), Worksop and Tamworth (for Bakers Nuts). Smiths had their own fleet of 99 wagons some 20 of which operated to Bishops Waltham. The livery was maroon with white lettering, and the vehicles were marked with the Bishops Waltham business, along with the other Hampshire

bases of the firm. Some are known to have survived into the early 1950s. The Bishops Waltham office was manned by a manager, foreman, loader, three drivers and mates and a female office clerk, some of whom were sent to Botley as required to deal with any work at that station. Three lorries were provided at Bishops Waltham but from about 1960 there were only two.

In 1879 some heated correspondence began between the London and South Western Railway and the Bishops Waltham Gas & Coke Company over the charges made for gas supplied to the station. A letter from the LSWR on 14th February complained that the rate charged (6/8d. per 1000 cubic feet) was too high and after consideration the Gas Company agreed to reduce their charge to 5/10d from 25th March. However, it appears the LSWR were still not satisfied and Mr. W. H. Stratton of the Stores Department wrote on the 24th February 1880:

> 'The Directors of this Company have again called my attention to the price you are charging for Gas supplied to Bishops Waltham station and I have been instructed to inform you that they consider it much too high and that unless you reduce it to 5/- per 1000 cu. ft. they must make other arrangements for lighting that station.'

In response the Gas Company Directors reluctantly agreed to reduce the charge to the requested charge of 5/- from 25th March 1880 and here matters rested until 25th August 1882 when the LSWR complained that charges were still too high and made a strong request for a further reduction. On this

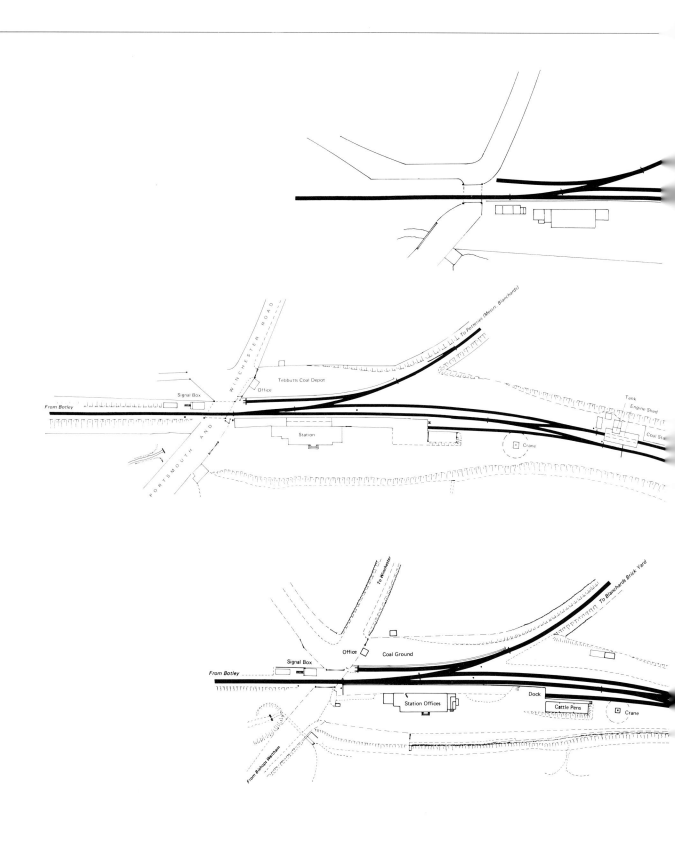

From Botley

WINCHESTER ROAD

PORTSMOUTH AND

Signal Box

Office

Tebbutts Coal Depot

To Potteries (Messrs. Blanchards)

Tank

Engine Shed

Coal Sta

Station

Crane

To Winchester

To Blanchards Brick Yard

Office

Coal Ground

Signal Box

From Botley

Station Offices

Dock

Cattle Pens

Crane

From Bishops Waltham

SCALE — Approx. 2 chains to 1 inch

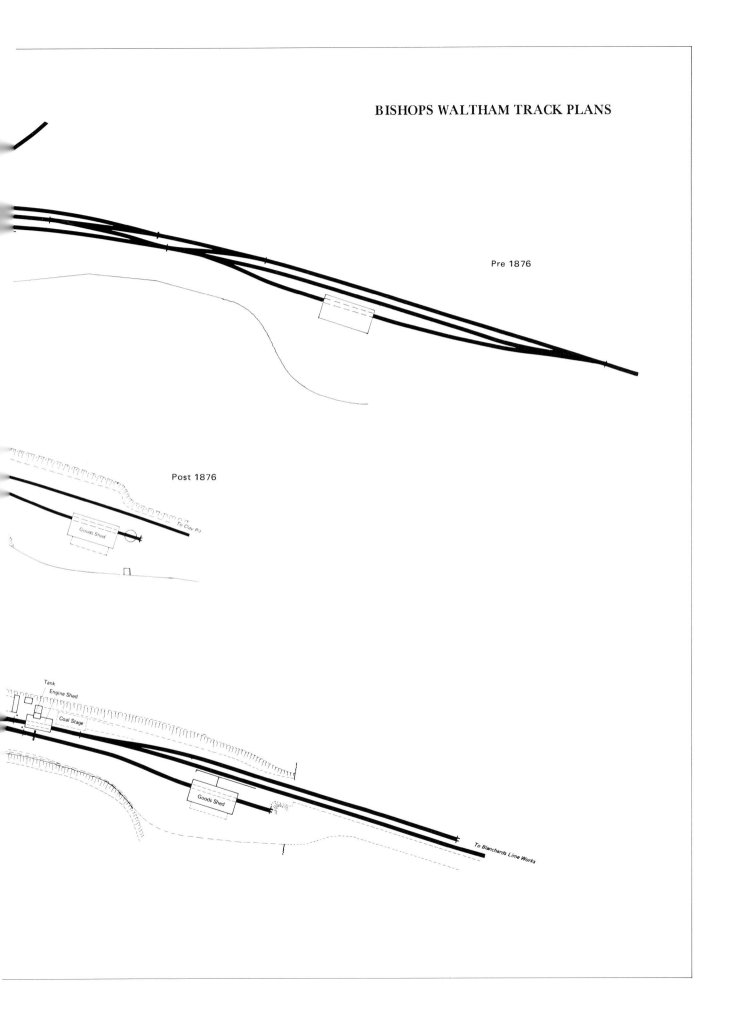

BISHOPS WALTHAM TRACK PLANS

Pre 1876

Post 1876

To Clay Pit

Goods Shed

Tank

Engine Shed

Coal Stage

Goods Shed

To Blanchards Lime Works

A post-1935 view, looking north following the removal of the signalbox. The crossing gates had been converted to hand operation at this time. Other features to disappear were the shunting bell and communication with the yard, the catch points in the station loop and the Dutton's shelter over the ground frame at Edwards Siding. The telephone in the signalbox was transferred to the crossing cottage at Durley. The site of the 1863 temporary station would have been close to where the photographer was standing.   LENS OF SUTTON

occasion the Gas Company decided to make further investigations and before replying wrote to neighbouring gas companies to ask what they were charging the LSWR. What influence the replies had is uncertain but on 29th September the Bishops Waltham G&CC resolved to refuse to alter their charges.

Unrepentant, the LSWR wrote on 2nd November 1885 stating in their opinion that 'in consideration of their large consumption of Gas, the Company were entitled to a reduction in price.' A somewhat curt reply was sent from the BWG&CC, refusing to consider any reduction and labouring the point that the LSWR were not their largest consumer. Following similar correspondence in 1888 between the two companies, matters came to a head on 21st October 1889 when the LSWR wrote:

'The price you are charging us for Gas at the Bishops Waltham Station being much higher than we are paying at the majority of Stations on this Railway, I hope you will be able to inform me in reply that you are prepared to make a substantial reduction as from the 29th Ultimo. Our arrangements for lighting certain Stations with Mineral Oil have proved most successful, I trust therefore you will offer to supply us with Gas in the future at such a rate as will prevent any change in the system of lighting the station above named'.

The risk of losing its income from the LSWR prompted the Gas Company to offer a discount of 10% to *all* consumers of gas whose annual consumption amounted to £20 and upwards and thereafter the matters appears to have finally rested and no

further reference to charges are recorded in either company's minute books.

The staffing of the station from the opening is unclear but it almost certainly came under the supervision of the Botley station master and this is known to have been the case from 1868. However, traffic had developed to such an extent by the turn of the century that Bishops Waltham was put under the separate control of a Class 4 station master, Charles Colbourne at a salary of £100 per annum. Mr. Colbourne was in residence until he retired in August 1919. During the 1920s the encumbent was Charles Blount who was paid a salary of £230 upon his appointment on 25th December 1921. Mr. Blount is recalled as being a dab hand at baking seed cakes, and a billiard fanatic prone to whistling as he played his shots!

When passenger services were withdrawn, Bishops Waltham again became the responsibility of the Botley station master and only one grade 1 goods porter was retained to deal with all the work. This included handling traffic, unloading, loading and sheeting wagons, checking and keeping up with paperwork. He was also responsible for the upkeep and locking/unlocking the station buildings and of course enquiries from traders. During the 1950s this job was filled by Jack Cattle, an elderly man, who caused a great deal of frustration to engine crews on the daily goods working. He is said to have been in the habit of forgetting to open the crossing gates when the train was due, and the continuous whistling of the engine was to no avail as Jack was stone deaf!. This unfortunate

The station building following closure to passenger traffic. The small canopy over the door to the booking office has been removed. Other internal changes included removing the partition between the waiting room and station master's office, the area being converted for dealing with parcels and goods to facilitate the letting of the goods shed. The station nameboard was removed and the front door of the station building was converted to serve the station house only. The small hut on the extreme right of the picture was used as an engineers' store.
R. M. CASSERLEY

The accommodation left to right was Gents' toilet (obscured by end of bus), lamp room, ladies' room and toilet, waiting room and booking office. The two-storey end was the private accommodation for the station master.
R. M. CASSERLEY

A 1960s view following removal of the station canopy. Today the station building would be regarded as a desirable residence. However, it is interesting to reflect on a proposal by the SR in July 1935 to convert the building into a 'residential flat', not proceeded with as 'there would probably be some difficulty in obtaining a tenant'.   LENS OF SUTTON

A companion photograph, showing the neglected appearance of the station in the final years. Closure had been considered in 1952 but traffic levels justified retention. Total annual receipts amounted to £24,941 with some 6,653 tons of merchandise and minerals and 5,420 tons of coal, coke and patent fuels. Parcels traffic amounted to 5,409 tons. Savings by closure of the branch were estimated at £6,476 per annum.   LENS OF SUTTON

An early photograph from the pond showing the engine and goods sheds. The style of the goods shed was very in keeping with the station building, but unlike the latter, it was constructed entirely in brick. The engine shed was an early casualty of the 1930s economies, the first consideration for closure coming in April 1931. The reduction in operating department staff was estimated at £400 per annum with a net reduction of 44 train miles, plus 42 light engine miles per week. COURTESY JOHN BOSWORTH

Following removal of the engine shed in July 1931, the water tank was retained at the insistence of the Locomotive Department. The wagons are standing on the goods shed road which by 1952 was truncated and the building leased out. The end loading dock, which also served the cattle pens, can be seen in front of the first wagon. W. A. CAMWELL

Bishops Waltham viewed from the north-east. The engine shed can be glimpsed in the top right-hand corner. The amount of goods traffic handled is evidenced by the large number of open wagons, many of which would have brought in coal for the local merchants and the gas works. The latter would receive small coal in vast quantities to maintain the three or four retorts in operation. Complete trains of coal for the gas works were not unknown. Pratts Motor Oil had a local distribution point close to the gas works where a large tank mounted on a brick base was replenished from rail tank wagons. These were pushed into position rather than being loose shunted.

AIR VIEWS LTD., AUTHORS' COLLECTION

Looking south over the end loading dock which formerly accommodated the cattle pens. The considerable volume of tail traffic in pre-war years resulted in the extension of the loading dock and the provision of three cattle pens provided in September 1914 at an estimated cost of £156. The pens were removed around the time of the cessation of the local cattle sales.   J. J. DAVIS

disability rendered the station office telephone useless and any messages had to be relayed in person by the Botley station master.

Although in decline, the amount of traffic in the post-war period was still appreciable, particularly coal and mill traffic. By 1956 the brickworks had ceased production, their siding already being out of use, but later, around 1958, part of the works site was taken over by Meon Valley Metals who used the railway for some outward movement of scrap metal. In fact one of their mobile road cranes was unofficially requisitioned by the railway staff on one occasion when an open wagon containing mill traffic for Messrs. Dukes became derailed in the yard during shunting. It seems a tarpaulin cover caught in a wheel and eventually caused it to come off the road. The enterprising engine crew and porter tried to re-rail the offending vehicle using the road crane but this ingenious attempt failed when the crane lifted off the ground instead! The Eastleigh breakdown gang subsequently put matters right with lifting jacks.

The daily goods service was officially reduced to a twice weekly event around 1961. During this period a carrier service was still offered by Eric Gregory of Eastleigh who served Bishops Waltham and Botley on alternate days with parcels

Since at least 1953 Dukes had rented the goods shed to store grain in sacks stacked against the internal walls of the building. By the 1960s the grain was stored loose and the quantities held had increased to a point when finally, sometime in 1964, the contents, some 300 tons at the time, became too much for the old building and the walls bowed out and caused the roof to fall in!

The water tank survived until final closure in 1962.   J. J. DAVIS

Looking north from the end of the loading dock towards the far end of the yard. During the Second World War military traffic, (including a variety of vehicles) was dealt with for the base at Hazelholt Park. Messrs. Houghton's Sawmills of Durley handled large quantities of timber here which they moved using a steam lorry. J. J. DAVIS

The shortened goods shed siding. J. J. DAVIS

The rather ornate goods shed, with a 5-ton crane mounted on the loading platform, was leased to Messrs. Duke & Son for the storage of grain. Shown here in June 1954, the building survived beyond the line's closure until the unfortunate incident in 1964. J. J. DAVIS

Open wagons at the far end of the yard awaiting attention. Coal merchants such as Messrs. King & Privett, Hulme of Upham and M. J. Davies, had wharves at this point but coal was generally shovelled direct into sacks and taken away almost straight away. The white building in front of the goods shed was used by Messrs. Scats as a grain store. Entry to this end of the yard was gained via a large gate at the end of Brooklands Road.

AUTHORS' COLLECTION

DURLEY

The daily goods service returning to Botley behind Class M7 0—4—4T No. 30375 on 12th January 1957. The platform of Durley Halt was situated alongside the train. Passenger traffic was always light; apart from the mill workers, a few schoolchildren travelled from here to Prices School in Fareham, and three or four shoppers on the afternoon services. With little patronisation by rail travellers, the small shelter on the platform was popular with local courting couples! Following passenger closure in 1933 the platform face was removed and the wall cut back to a 1 in 1½ slope. The shelter, three lamps and the wicket gates on the down side were removed. The lamp box was transferred to Bishops Waltham. During World War II an air raid shelter was located at the back of the north platform slope. In earlier times the crossing apparently bore an array of notices including at least one for the guidance of owners of traction engines. Traffic over the crossing was mainly farm vehicles with some horse vans from Durley Mill, pony traps and commercial delivery vans. A. W. BURGESS

The village of Durley is situated some three miles from Bishops Waltham in the midst of a network of country lanes. The old Roman road passing through the area from Portchester to Winchester is still just traceable, and the manor house, dating from around the time of Henry VII, is noteworthy for its 'continental appearance'.

In 1901 the population of Durley was 510, the railway passing a mile or so from the village, crossing the old road leading from Durley Mill across Breach Hill. Probably from the opening or soon after, the crossing was manned by a gatekeeper, but on 27th April 1881 the L&SW approved the construction of a rent free cottage for a platelayer whose wife could undertake the duty, thus saving a gatekeeper's wage. Soon after the introduction of the railmotor service, the inhabitants of the area, led by the Scivier family who ran the nearby Mill, were pressing the L&SW to provide a halt at Durley Mill crossing. On 16th August 1905 the company considered the matter, having identified the estimated cost of £44. However, the matter did not proceed further until a second attempt was made to coerce the LSWR, the directors approving the provision of a platform at an estimated cost of £67 on 4th November 1909.

Major Pringle inspected the work for the Board of Trade on 24th January 1910:

'I made an inspection today of the new works at Durley between Botley and Bishops Waltham on the London and South Western Railway. A new platform has been constructed on the north side of the single line about 2¼ miles south-west of Bishops Waltham. The platform has a length of 120 feet, a width of about 8 feet and is raised 3 feet above rail level. It is properly fenced and lighted and access is provided from the adjoining public road level crossing by means of a ramp. Nameboards "Durley Halt" have been fixed. There is no shelter and no signals have been provided.'

He approved the opening of the halt to the public on the understanding that 'further accommodation would be provided if such should be found necessary'. It can only be assumed that the Major was referring to a shelter for passengers. The halt had been brought into use on 23rd December 1909 and Harry Elliot is remembered as the man who gave the first 'all clear' on that day.

The *South-Western Gazette* reported in January 1910 'the number of passengers using the Halt fully comes up to expectation' and no doubt encouraged by this fact, approval was given on 3rd November 1910 to provide a wooden shelter at an estimated cost of £35.

Although the station was distant from Durley village, it was conveniently placed to serve the hamlets of Calcot and Frogmill. The modest but steady passenger traffic consisted mainly of local shopping trips to Bishops Waltham and Botley, schoolchildren and workers at the nearby Mill. It was not unknown for crews to offer a 'personal' service whereby a particular train might make an unofficial stop at Calcot Bridge

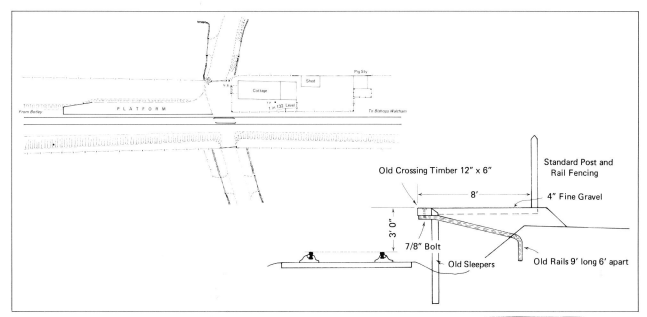

or elsewhere in the Durley area to set down a passenger or two who lived close at hand and save them a walk across the fields from the halt.

Facilities for handling goods were considered in 1912 by means of a siding at Calcot bridge costing £900 including the purchase of additional land from a Dr. Maybury. The provision of a siding here was originally suggested in 1862 but not proceeded with when the line was built. It was later discussed by the L&SW in December 1910 following a request from Mr. E. Swinstead, a fruit grower, on behalf of himself and others. They were to guarantee a minimum traffic of 2,800 tons per annum or, if not achieved, a payment of 6d per ton on the goods received and despatched which was assumed to amount to £70 per annum. The cost of the siding had then been estimated at £600. The reason for the delay in undertaking the work was due to difficulty in purchasing the necessary land. A revised plan was submitted increasing the estimated cost to that referred to.

Some uncertainty exists as to whether the work was proceeded with. Official records do not make further reference to the siding and personal recollections are conflicting as to whether it was ever constructed. However, a descendant of the mill owners confirms that their traffic was always dealt with at Botley and remembers that correspondence with the L&SWR over the siding came to nothing. This tends to be confirmed by the Working Timetable Appendix for 1921 which makes no mention of a siding at this location.

As previously mentioned, from 1881 the wife of one of the permanent way staff was responsible for the operation of the crossing gates and remarkably this stayed in the one family from the outset to the early 1950s. The first occupants of the crossing keeper's cottage were a Mr. & Mrs. Elliott, Mr. Elliott having worked on the construction of the railway. From 1907 their daughter Alice assumed responsibilities for the crossing and remained here until her retirement in April 1954. In 1927 Alice, then Mrs. Tubbs, took on additional responsibilities when the train guard was withdrawn from the passenger services on the branch. She had to meet each train, handle any parcels traffic and light and extinguish the three station oil lamps. From 1954 the cost of opening and closing the gates fell to the train guard on the daily goods service.

The railway clock provided in the cottage was subsequently removed and taken to Botley. It was unusual in being an ex-LBSCR clock said to have originated from the No. 1 platform at Brighton and in remarkably good condition.

A late 19th-century scene in Durley brickworks. Durley was one of a numerous scattering of small brickworks in Hampshire totalling some 150 or so. A range of clay-based products emerged from these works including roofing tiles, floor tiles, drain pipes, bricks of various types and sizes and other domestic items. Durley brickworks was managed by a Mr. Church at the time this photograph was taken and is known to have supplied bricks to the LSWR for the construction of the Meon Valley line in 1900/1. HAMPSHIRE COUNTY MUSEUM SERVICE

A well-known postcard view of Botley in the Edwardian era. The railmotor is in the Bishops Waltham bay, and the branch itself can be seen disappearing to the right under the roadbridge. Notice the porter climbing the Up Starting signal to replenish the lamp.

AUTHORS' COLLECTION

BOTLEY

Station Road Botley

Station Road, looking towards Curdridge in the early years of the century. The Railway Hotel is seen on the extreme right, with the approach road to the station disappearing off to the left. Many years ago a local resident who travelled on the first excursion train to leave Botley stated that 'the train bound for London had passengers crowded into carriages like cattle trucks, without any kind of covering and some had come in from a great distance to join the train from the new station'.   COURTESY JACK TICKNER

Botley was described in 1907 as a small town pleasantly situated on the Hamble River, at that time navigable for barges up to that point. The Romans had a settlement close by at Fairthorne and later a place was referred to in Anglo-Saxon times as Botelei. It is said that the town was almost certainly burnt by the Danes in the year 1001 as the remains of a 130 ft galley was discovered deep in the mud of the Hamble between Bursledon and Botley. William Cobbett had been a resident here for many years and during this period was instrumental in the construction of the turnpike through Twyford to Winchester. The town had been brought into prominence by the opening of a new bridge over the river around 1839 and the same year also saw the passing of the Bill for a proposed railway from Bishopstoke to Gosport in Parliament.

This line, promoted by the then London and Southampton Railway Company, was to leave the main line at Bishopstoke and head eastward by way of Botley and Fareham to Gosport, thus opening up the Portsmouth and Isle of Wight traffic. Not all those in Botley and the surrounding area were in favour of the railway and the prosperity it would bring, and some opposition was launched particularly from individuals with a commercial interest in the stage coaches and the profitable farming land. However, this was overcome and the new line opened on 29th November 1841.

The construction had not been without its problems; the mixture of clays and sand stretching from Southampton Water and the Hamble Estuary caused the contractor Thomas Brassey difficulties in finding firm ground and levels in the Botley area. During the construction of the station it was found necessary to sink numerous wooden piles to get a foundation for the station buildings. These problems were to manifest themselves in later years as many slips occurred in the cuttings approaching the station and much shoring up took place, particularly in the 1930s. However, the notorious Fareham tunnel north of that station presented the line's main obstacle with numerous problems owing to the instability of the sub soil clay beds. The opening had been postponed from July to enable a collapse to be remedied. Against the advice of the Board of Trade inspector, the November opening went ahead, only to prove four days later that the advice was well founded as further slips rendered the tunnel unsafe for passenger working. Major repairs were thus put into effect including opening out the affected cutting and approach slopes to the northern portal. Following another Board of Trade inspection, the line was re-opened for passenger traffic on 7th February 1842.

Botley station was located about $\frac{3}{4}$ mile east of the town and was in fact in the parish of Curdridge. It became a junction on 1st June 1863 with the opening of the branch to Bishops

Fruit Trains leaving Station, Botley.

Botley was transformed during the strawberry season with much frenzied activity to ensure the fruit was dealt with as quickly as possible. Here a fruit special is waiting to depart behind a pair of Adams 4-4-0s. The Class O2 0-4-4T, having arrived with the goods service from Bishops Waltham, is waiting to cross to the yard. The remainder of its train is stood on the branch running line. The sidings held about 25-28 wagons each and there was a 30 cwt crane in the yard. Yard buildings supplementing the goods shed were a checker's office and coal office (near the goods shed), a wooden hut at the end of the yard (gone by 1953) used by Timothy Whites to store chemicals and medicines, and a fruit office near the station platform.
LENS OF SUTTON

Waltham. A new bay platform was constructed on the down side with provision for an independent access to the station. The station master at this time was James Whitney who, at least by February 1868, had assumed responsibilities for Bishops Waltham as well, for which the L&SW increased his annual salary from £110 to £120. During Mr. Whitney's tenure of office he had frequent cause to write to his employers on matters which serve to highlight some of the finer points of his conditions. On 14th June 1860 Mr. Whitney was successful in persuading the L&SW to stop charging him £1 rental per annum for his garden and the following year he sought to have the charge for income tax on his house stopped. Whether he was successful in this matter is not recorded.

The traffic handled developed very rapidly from the opening of the station, early patronage stemming from the nearby flour mills. Timber and farm produce, including livestock movements, were another common feature. It did not take long for the numerous fruit growers scattered thereabouts in this part of the county to realise the potential of the railway to transport their highly perishable products rapidly to market centres up and down the country. Such is the importance of this aspect of traffic at Botley that it is dealt with separately.

By the middle to late 1870s, facilities for both passenger and goods traffic were becoming inadequate for the rapid growth in patronage. Requests by residents for additional waiting accommodation in September 1875 were finally sanctioned by the LSWR in December 1884 when a shelter (presumably the wooden canopy extension shown in Appendix 9) and a footbridge was provided at an estimated cost of £235. Further agitation in the form of a memorial to the LSWR in 1889 resulted in the company approving the provision of additional waiting rooms and urinal accommodation in February 1890 at an estimated cost of £723. However plans for the provision of a waiting room on the down platform were not proceeded with. Later in September 1915 internal structural changes within the station house were effected, improving and enlarging the booking office and providing better access to the Ladies waiting room, the cost of this work being estimated at £39.

Accommodation for handling goods traffic appears to have been criticised by several traders from about 1880. Mill traffic had increased appreciably since the opening of the line, although two requests from Messrs. W.&J. Clarke Flour Mills, in June 1880 for the erection of a goods warehouse and in August 1883 for an additional siding were declined by an apparently reticent LSWR. However, pressure from the numerous fruit growers for improvements to the yard mileage were more successful, as described later.

The farms in the locality provided a regular source of revenue in the form of seasonal produce and regular livestock movements including brood mares. 'Round' timber and chemical products, mainly insecticides, from Messrs. Murphy were also dealt with. Coal merchants receiving coal products at the station around the turn of the century were Messrs. D. A. Bell, who also dealt in corn and manure, and Messrs. W. & J. Clarke. By 1915 Mr. James Butt was trading at the station. He is known to have owned his own wagons although no further details are known. By the 1930s these earlier firms seem to have disappeared as the wharf leases had been taken by Messrs. T. Brown, Botley Flour Milling Co., Roxburgh & Scivier and J. E. Smith (Portsmouth) Ltd. The latter firm had their office at Bishops Waltham and only received some coal at Botley for

local delivery from about 1921. They later opened an office at Botley in 1962 when the branch closed. Photographic evidence and staff recollections both fail to reveal the existence of any coal offices in the yard. Roxburgh & Scivier are known to have had their office at a garage which they also ran. No cart weighbridge was provided in the yard as one was available in the village.

Shunting activity in the yard, almost certainly in preparation for a short working to Eastleigh. Wagons destined for or returning from Bishops Waltham were marshalled to form with the stopping goods services on the Fareham to Eastleigh line.
JOHN KING COLLECTION

FRUIT TRAFFIC

The area around Botley and Swanwick has for many years been the centre of the soft fruit growing region of Hampshire. An impression of the scale of the activity can be gleaned from evidence that the District Fruit Growers Association during the early years of the century had over 600 growers on its register. The main crop was strawberries and the opening of the railway in 1841 provided the growers with the considerable advantage of rapid transport to the markets for their highly perishable product. A mutual prosperity thus ensued and the seasonal traffic developed at a considerable pace.

In general, the strawberry season, although very brief, provided the LSWR with a considerable volume of traffic. Over one million baskets of the fruit were handled in one season, about 400 baskets to the ton. All of this was forwarded from ten stations, namely Botley, Swanwick, Bursledon, Netley, Sholing, Bitterne, Fareham, Wickham, Eastleigh and Romsey.

From the start of each season it was necessary for the LSWR to make special arrangements to cope with the sudden surge of traffic. As the weather was paramount in determining the picking of the fruit, the company maintained close touch with the growers who reported on the ripening of the strawberries. A hot sunny May could cause the fruit to be ready for market several weeks earlier than usual. A good season could result in a bumper crop like 1904 when a record 1,500,000 baskets were dealt with. At least some advance notice of these situations was vital for the additional preparations to be made.

An additional siding to deal with this traffic, was approved on 15th October 1884 at an estimated cost of £1,965, this figure suggesting the works were fairly substantial. The work described as 'being urgently required' was put in hand immedi-

389
BOTLEY STATION.
1907

A typical June scene in pre-war years with an interesting variety of LNWR, Midland and LSWR vans amongst those present. The large wicker baskets in the foreground had superseded orange boxes which had proved unsatisfactory as much fruit was damaged. The smaller 'chip' baskets also seen here held 3lb or 4lb of fruit, dependent upon size. These replaced the larger 'gallon' baskets when the railway companies were persuaded by the growers' associations to provide racking or shelving in their vans. Owing to space restrictions, children were usually employed to pack the vans and they were paid 3d per hour. Such were the numbers involved that the local school holiday was timed to coincide with the picking season.

Horse-drawn carts were by far the most common means of transporting the highly perishable fruit to the station, although traction engines and hand-carts were also used. The carts, as seen here, were fitted with wire racks and wooden shelving in order to maximise capacity. At the height of the season, carts would be arriving and departing from dawn till dusk, long queues could develop back up the station approach sometimes up to half a mile away. As a result of this seasonal traffic, the station approach was widened in 1892 to relieve bottlenecks. COURTESY JACK TICKNER

The hours were both long and hard for pickers, growers and railwaymen alike. Starting at 5 a.m. or thereabouts, picking would continue unabated until about 9 p.m. Whole families were involved in the process, providing an annual opportunity to supplement normal meagre incomes from agricultural work. Strawberry growing created additional traffic for the LSWR through the growers' need for high quantities of straw and good quality dung! COURTESY JACK TICKNER

Another scene of unabated activity in 1907. Such was the volume of strawberry traffic in the Botley/Bursledon/Swanwick areas that the LSWR instituted special strawberry train arrangements each year. During the peak years of this traffic on one day, 29th June 1923, 64 loaded vans left Botley containing 66,017 baskets of fruit with carriage charges for the SR of £571 19s 0d. Shelving tended to be provided in most vans from about 1898, an assortment of vacuum-fitted and dual-fitted vehicles being used, mainly 6-wheelers. To cope with the demand, the LSWR built or converted many vans in the years around the turn of the century. In 1915 three million baskets of strawberries were despatched from the Hampshire growing area.

LENS OF SUTTON

A welcome break for the horses while unloading takes place. Less caring drivers would overwork the horses and, with the constant pressure to get the fruit to the station, occasions of horses dropping dead on Calcot Hill have been recorded. The distances varied but many growing fields were located at least two miles from the station as the fruit area was on the opposite side of the village. Owing to the delicate nature of the fruit, growers were reluctant to use local carriers and usually insisted that their own employees loaded the strawberries direct into the railway vans. Railway staff concentrated on the checking and waybill duties. The LNWR, GWR, MR and GC Companies sent inspectors to Botley to advise LSWR staff with regard to loading and transhipment of their own vans.

COURTESY JACK TICKNER

ately. Later, in March 1907, further improvements were requested by the Growers Association and Curdridge Parish Council for handling facilities in the yard. The LSWR responded in May by slewing an existing siding and adding another and a new cartway at an estimated cost of £1,060. These works were brought into use in June.

Traffic at this time had reached a zenith which lasted well into the 1930s. The 1906 season had seen some 1,500 tons of strawberries grown in the district, of which 1,013 tons 7 cwt were dealt with at Botley, requiring on some days up to 60 vans to convey the fruit to London and the markets in the north of England. An average of some 30,000 baskets were despatched daily from the station.

Such was the activity that only three years after the previous works the LSWR General Manager recommended on 28th April 1910 'that another siding and carting space for handling fruit traffic at Botley can be provided at an estimated cost of £2,570.' It is not clear whether this cost included the extension of the overbridge at the end of the yard (undertaken at the same time), but this, coupled with the purchase of additional land (1 rod, 8 perches) from Mr. Arthur Jenkyns, enabled the existing sidings to be slewed and lengthened. Each siding could

subsequently accommodate about 26 vans. These works were brought into use in April 1911.

The frenzied activity abounding in the few weeks of the season required the drafting in of extra staff from various parts of the railway network.

Some of these staff came from metropolitan stations and yards in the London area and it was not uncommon for the hard pressed station staff to work through from 8 a.m. to 9 p.m. or 10 p.m. loading and marshalling vehicles ready for departure. Van loads destined for the markets in the Midlands and the North would usually depart during the afternoon, and those for London (Nine Elms goods depot) in early or mid-evening. Strawberries were sent as far afield as Glasgow and Edinburgh and vehicles with this traffic were attached to a morning service originating from Swanwick, going by way of Fareham. Most of the larger towns in the Midlands and the North received large quantities of strawberries including Liverpool, Manchester, Birmingham, Leeds and towns in Wales and Ireland.

Facilities for the influx of the short term extra staff engaged in the season were provided but these were described by the LSWR General Manager in 1919 as 'very meagre and inad-

A c.1920 view of the station staff supplemented by temporary workers for the strawberry season. Extra staff were transferred from other stations and short term casuals were hired. The station master is Mr. Herbert Wright-Jones and to his right is Mr. Cook, Messrs. W. H. Smith & Son's bookstall attendant.
BOTLEY & CURDRIDGE LOCAL HISTORY SOCIETY

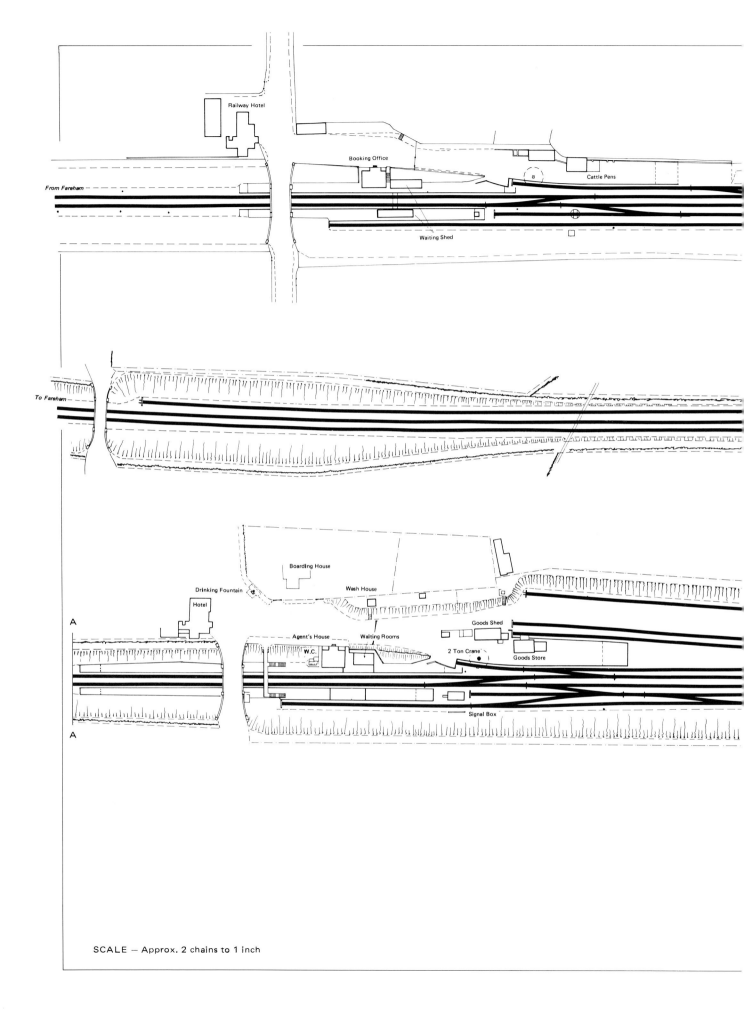

From Fareham

Railway Hotel

Booking Office

Waiting Shed

Cattle Pens

To Fareham

A

Hotel

Drinking Fountain

Boarding House

Wash House

Agent's House

W.C.

Waiting Rooms

Goods Shed

2 Ton Crane

Goods Store

Signal Box

A

SCALE — Approx. 2 chains to 1 inch

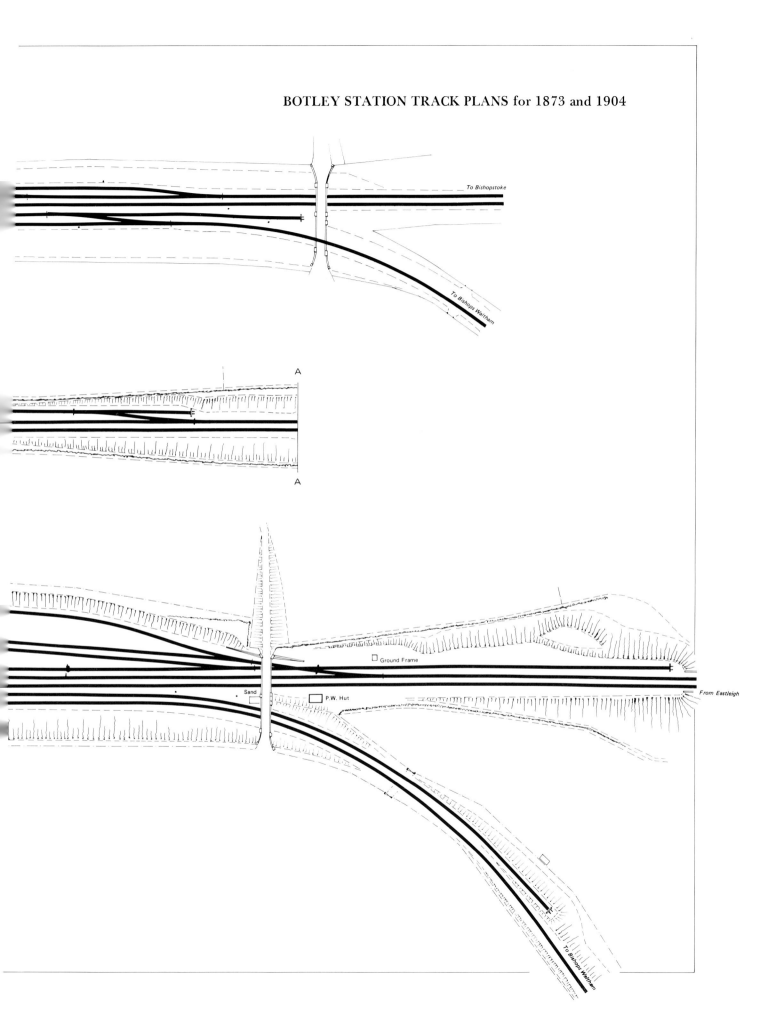

BOTLEY STATION TRACK PLANS for 1873 and 1904

To Bishopstoke

To Bishops Waltham

A

A

Ground Frame

Sand

P.W. Hut

From Eastleigh

To Bishops Waltham

A rare picture to come to light of railmotor No. 1 in the bay, taken between October and November 1904 when No. 1 was transferred to the Plymouth area. The introduction of railcars in October 1904 prompted the eventual re-introduction of the Sunday service on the branch from 1st April 1906, providing five return trips. The redoubtable guard George Padwick is seen just to the left of the lamp.

BOTLEY & CURDRIDGE LOCAL HISTORY SOCIETY

A Portsmouth-bound train entering Botley on 7th November 1928 behind 'K10' 4–4–0 No. E341. The western end of the station was prone to occasional flooding, one notable occurrence on 24th September 1924 caused some disruption to services.   H. C. CASSERLEY

equate'. Improvements were made in May of that year when at a cost of £44 the loft area over the goods shed was converted to a suitable shelter and rest area for the men.

Some of the growers who regularly carted strawberries to the station are recalled as Messrs. Gordon Reed, Frank Abraham, Rickman Brothers, Page & Sons and A. E. Roberts who brought his wares from Wickham. Swanmore based growers also used Botley, Messrs. Watsons, House and Green being among those remembered carting from their fields. Of the different varieties grown in the area, the ones most frequently handled at Botley were 'Climax', 'Cambridge Favourite' and 'Red Gauntlet'.

From the mid 1930s, when an outbreak of red core disease hit the area, the strawberry traffic around Botley went into a steady decline. The main growing area then shifted further eastward, concentrating on Swanwick. However, despite the fall in output, the mid 1950s still saw around 15 vanloads a day during the peak period of the season.

An incident occurred sometime in the 1950s when a van loaded with fruit derailed during the shunting of the evening London-bound strawberry train. Another vehicle was hurriedly found and the staff had to work late into the evening transferring the load from the offending vehicle.

INCIDENTS

A few minor incidents around the station area have been recorded over the years, the first being on 24th June 1921 when at 2.30 p.m. a hut in the yard was totally destroyed by fire. Believed to have been caused by a spark from the shunting engine working the yard, the LSWR reported 'In view that the female checkers for whose convenience the hut was pro-

vided are not now employed at Botley, it is not proposed to replace the structure.'

On 4th July 1932 at about 1.40 p.m. a 'D1' class engine, possibly No. B240, derailed at the points leading from the up line to the up sidings, thereby blocking the up line, and necessitated single line working between Eastleigh and Botley until 3.30 p.m. The engine had been performing the day's service on the branch and was being used to shunt some fruit vans in the yard. The 2.05 p.m. service to Bishops Waltham and the return 3.05 p.m. return trip were cancelled, passengers being conveyed by road. It later transpired that the derailment was the result of a misunderstanding between the relief signalman and the driver of the engine who had not waited for a hand signal.

As already mentioned on page 51, the railway cutting to the east of the station was prone to landslips. In the mid-1930s major shifts in the strata occurred requiring a considerable amount of remedial work by the civil engineering staff. The first slip occurred at 4.40 a.m. on 29th November 1935 in the cutting on the down side of the line between the down starting and advance starting signals. The Engineer was given possession of the down line at 7.45 p.m. until the following morning to put matters right. At 6.35 a.m. on 30th November the engine of a 'materials' train provided for loading and removing earth, derailed while propelling a wagon towards the station owing to further subsidence. The unfortunate engine was eventually rerailed at 9.28 a.m.

At 8.10 a.m. further movements rendered the up line blocked and unsafe to use. All train services were then diverted via Netley until 4.30 p.m. when single line working on the up line came into force between Knowle Junction and Botley. This

The major landslip which occurred on 8th January 1936. Here remedial work is shown in progress on clearing the way for the re-opening of the down line to traffic. The bank was cut back significantly to avoid future trouble.   COURTESY JACK TICKNER

Manual effort supplemented by an ancient-looking excavator makes good nature's destruction. The open wagon on the left appears to be an old North Eastern specimen with grease boxes.   COURTESY JACK TICKNER

Single line working was in force on the up line from 9th January.   COURTESY JACK TICKNER

The clearing work nearly complete, although it was some time before both up and down lines were available again. It was believed locally that the work on the new graving dock at Southampton had affected underground streams and the change in the water table caused the series of landslips at Botley.

COURTESY JACK TICKNER

Station Road and the Railway Hotel in 1964, looking towards the village of Botley about three-quarters of a mile away. As Curdridge was close by, in March 1904 the parish council sought to have the name of that village added to the name of the station. However, the LSWR declined.
                                                                                    HAMPSHIRE CHRONICLE

The station forecourt in 1964. The entrance on the right was the private entry to the station master's accommodation. Public access to the station was via the archway on the left leading down steps to the station platform. The building in front of the up starting signal was originally used as the fruit traffic office, but with the post-war decline it was taken over by Murphy Chemicals around 1950.
                                                                                    HAMPSHIRE CHRONICLE

arrangement continued until 12.30 p.m. on 5th December when the engineering staff relinquished possession of the down line and moved over to the up line for further remedial work. However, this did not last long as at 7.45 a.m. the following day the down line again became blocked, forcing the hard pressed Engineer to move back again. Double line working did not finally resume until 10 a.m. on 10th December with a 5 m.p.h. speed restriction in force in both directions.

This was not to be the end of the trouble, however, as 16th December saw a minor slip which, although causing concern, did not interrupt train services. It was by now becoming a major headache for the Botley permanent way gang who were forced to keep an almost constant vigil in the problem stretch. The land movement of the 16th was only a prelude to a serious slip in the cutting at around 10 p.m. on 21st December rendering the down line out of action. Single line working over the up line came into force, lasting intermittently throughout the repair work until 8th January 1936 when another major slip blocked the down line completely again. On this occasion

Station forecourt and entry to the yard in the early 1950s, with a splendid looking Alvis outside the station house. In May 1944 King George VI stayed overnight at the station in the royal train.
HARRY NEWMAN

This view was taken from the footbridge in 1964, looking towards Eastleigh. The main facilities on the up side consisted of a combined booking and parcels office, general and ladies waiting rooms and station master's office. Messrs. W. H. Smith & Son had a bookstall at the foot of the steps to the platform, and this was later run by Messrs. Simms. The living accommodation was all located on the first floor of the station house with the exception of a ground floor toilet. In 1899 there was a proposal to add a second floor providing two bedrooms, landing and cupboard, but this was not carried out.
HAMPSHIRE CHRONICLE

Botley station, photographed on 26th June 1953, after the closure of the branch to passengers. The rather neat wooden shelter on the down platform seems to have existed from the earliest days, but no mention or date appears in the minute books.   H. C. CASSERLEY

Another later photograph showing evidence of some rebuilding work to the down shelter.   LENS OF SUTTON

A general view from the bay in pre-nationalisation days. The footbridge was originally open, but following a memorial from local residents in March 1894, in September that year the LSWR agreed to undertake covering at an estimated cost of £180.
AUTHORS' COLLECTION

A 1964 photograph showing the replacement of the oil lamps with concrete post electric lamps undertaken c.1959. The footbridge is once again uncovered, the roof having been removed around 1955 at the request of the then station master Harry Newman as the wooden window frames on the sides were extensively rotten. The parapet walls were subsequently raised in height by some 8 or 9 inches. The six oil lamps removed from the footbridge had originally been in use at Itchen Abbas.
HAMPSHIRE CHRONICLE

Botley in the 1960s with the bay platform road having seen little recent use.

LENS OF SUTTON

the up line was also considered unsafe for the passing of trains and all services from Eastleigh to Fareham were diverted via St. Denys and the Netley line. Although the up line was re-opened at 6 p.m. the following day with single line working, remedial work on shoring up the cutting on the down side continued for several weeks, necessitating the purchase of a two acre strip of land from a C.B. Conybeare for £1,500 at the end of January. The down line was eventually re-opened just before

Easter after which the problems would finally seem to have been overcome as the minute books do not refer again to the matter.

OTHER WORKS

A refuge siding, provided on the up side east of the station in March 1893, was further extended in May 1894 at an estimated cost of £155. By 1905 it was found necessary to provide a

Botley signal box was of a standard LSWR design of the 1870s period tailored to local needs. In its earliest days the box had valancing around the bottom edge of the roof but, like many similar 'boxes, this was later removed post-1912. Notice there is no window to the locking frame room.

J. J. DAVIS

The branch diverged from the main line at the road-bridge west of the station. The bridge over the main line was originally a brick arch but was replaced by the girder span seen here to enable the yard to be extended. Additional siding accommodation was provided in November 1877, July 1897 and March 1907 at estimated costs of £500, £866 and £1,060 respectively. SEAN BOLAN

The signal box and the usual signalman's bicycle seen from a passing up train. The crossover from the branch was provided in September 1887 to enable the branch engine to run around its train. It was provided at an estimated cost of £58 and was operated from levers 18 and 19, the latter for the facing point lock.
LENS OF SUTTON

crossover road at this point 'carried out in connection with the abolition of tow-roping' according to the official inspection by Major Pringle for the Board of Trade on 14th April. A down advanced starting signal was also provided to control movements through the crossover from the up to the down line, together with a new ground signal for movements in the opposite direction. At the time Botley signal box was described as having an old frame of 30 levers.

During the course of the Second War some military traffic was evidently dealt with at Botley as in July 1943, the down siding parallel to the branch was extended at an estimated cost of £837 payable by the Government. At the same time the crossover opposite the signal box was moved to a new position 111 yards further west. Later, on 4th September 1944, a 9 inch thick concrete slab was laid at the end of the loading dock for a turning area for tanks. The costs of £480 was also met by Government funds.

STAFF

As already mentioned, the station master at Botley was also responsible for Bishops Waltham, that is apart from a period roughly from 1900 to 1930 when the latter station justified its

own position. The station master position was a Class 3 post which commanded an annual salary of £100 in 1910. This had increased by 1921 to £260 for Mr. Herbert W. Jones, who had taken the position on 26th March 1917. He is remembered as a somewhat pompous character who wore a bowler hat to greet the 'fast' trains. The station master was required to live in the station house for which he paid rent. In 1921 this amounted to £20 per annum and by the 1950s the method of assessment was based upon 15% of the annual salary.

By the 1930s the station staff consisted of 2 junior clerks, 3 signalmen, 2 grade 1 porters and a checker. The local carrier operating from the station in the early years was a Mr. Bastable, but by the turn of the century the Court family were offering this service, and after the First War a Mr. Hargreaves. Later the service was provided by Arthur Paskins and a Mr. Hill who both served Bishops Waltham. Local deliveries of parcels and other smalls were also undertaken by the station staff on a bicycle provided.

A permanent way gang of five men based at the station looked after the branch and a section of the main line. For 48 years, from about 1901, the ganger was Arthur Pragnall.

The typical 1950s goods train on its way to Bishops Waltham behind Class 'M7' 0–4–4T No. 30480. Later in the decade the service was shown in the timetables as running if required. This view, taken between Durley and Bishops Waltham, shows evidence of fresh ballasting and a standard of permanent way befitting a passenger-carrying line! A meeting of the Southern Region Branch Lines Committee in October 1952 had considered the future of the line but goods traffic levels were found to justify retention.
L. ELSEY

CHAPTER FIVE

'THE GOODS SERVICE'
1933 to 1962

FROM Monday, 2nd January 1933, the Bishops Waltham branch could no longer boast a passenger service. The character of the line changed completely and the twice-daily goods working did little to dispel the overwhelming impression that the line itself was moribund and derelict. The terminus, however, was little changed as for many years it had been goods traffic that had kept the line open, rather than the constantly declining few passengers.

A few days after the closure to passengers, a lorry ran out of control down Winchester Road and hit the rear of Bishops Waltham Signal Box. The damage, however, was somewhat minimal.

In December 1935 the SR reported that the signal box at Bishops Waltham would close with effect from the 16th of that month. All signals on the branch were removed and points converted to hand operation, at the same time the obsolete tablet instruments (which had been disconnected in July 1931) were taken away and put into store. The level crossing gates were changed to hand operation and locked by a two-lever ground frame. Only one signal post survived at Bishops Waltham – the down fixed distant, to which a lamp was added 'to enable enginemen to locate their position' (the official reason given). The fixed distant outside Botley station also remained.

THE OUTBREAK OF WAR

The second period of hostilities did not have an immediate effect on the branch, although ultimately it probably was of greater consequence than 25 years before. During the air raids on the strategic ports of Portsmouth and Southampton in the latter part of 1940, the area around Botley suffered a number of incidents. The first reported occasion was on 24th November when at 12.30 a.m. a bomb fell some 15 feet from the branch between the $\frac{1}{2}$ and $\frac{3}{4}$ mile posts (from Botley) and failed to explode. The line was declared 'blocked' and all services to Bishops Waltham were suspended until the bomb was successfully defused by an Army Bomb Disposal officer who authorised the line clear again at 2.30 p.m. the following day.

Having arrived at Bishops Waltham, No. 30480 is seen shunting a coal wagon into the back siding for J. E. Smith. The vans have been left in the platform to be dealt with by the goods porter.
L. ELSEY

No. 30480 manoeuvres vans into the north yard. At this time the private sidings had fallen into virtual disuse, no sign of activity on Blanchards or the Gas Works siding being recalled from about 1953. The last working remembered into the latter may have been pre-war when bogie wagons carrying large metal plates in connection with the erection of a large gasometer took place.

L. ELSEY

Having completed shunting duties, the empties and vehicles loaded with outgoing traffic have been collected and No. 30480 returns to Botley yard where the stock will be picked up by the stopping goods.   L. ELSEY

The intensified bombing of Portsmouth was, oddly enough, to increase the traffic on the branch, for when Messrs. Timothy White's main Portsmouth warehouse was razed, the company moved into temporary residence at Swanmore House ($3\frac{1}{2}$ miles from Botley) for about three years. Large volumes of merchandise were then handled at both Botley and Bishops Waltham. Parcels and small goods were dealt with at the latter station, with bulky or heavy goods at the former.

As the campaign intensified, Hazelholt Park, to the northeast of Bishops Waltham, was taken over by the Royal Engineers. A large materials store was established there and military accoutrements were brought in by rail to Bishops Waltham. During the peak of this traffic, an average of one train a day brought in materials such as 'dannett' wire, pickets and steel hawsers, all believed to have been intended for the home defence following the Dunkirk evacuation. At the terminus all materials were handled by military personnel and transported to the dump. For the duration of the RE's presence in the area, the station master's office accommodation was taken over and visible evidence of military activity at the station was provided by a REME workshop located at the far end of the yard.

By 1944 the REs had vacated Hazelholt Park to make way for American servicemen who took over the house. Here a large fuel storage area was planned as part of the overall strategy for the build-up to the invasion of Europe. Considerable quantities of petrol, aviation fuel and lubricants were brought in by rail, mostly in fifty gallon containers and often requiring up to two trains daily. The handling of this bulky traffic was eased by the American Military who increased the area of hard standing in the yard by infilling part of the pond.

Following the 'D' Day Campaign, the store at Hazelholt Park was dismantled, but the branch was to serve one final use during the hostilities – a holding point for empty tank wagons. The whole line, in effect, was treated as a long siding with wagons, colour coded according to the type of fuel carried, stretched out the full four miles from Botley to Bishops Waltham. Shunting requirements to remove or add vehicles was undertaken at night when strings of wagons were pulled out along the down line at Botley while single line working was in force over the up line to maintain services. Obviously this arrangement precluded any services over the branch, all traffic normally dealt with at Bishops Waltham being transferred to Botley yard.

Following the return to peace, the daily goods train resumed over the branch and continued uninterrupted (the service had reduced from two daily trips in the 1930s). Even the Nationalisation of January 1948 did not result in any immediate changes to the Bishops Waltham line, the Railway Executive was seemingly a million miles from this small corner of Hampshire.

One bright spot to bring back memories of the erstwhile passenger service occurred on 14th June 1952 when the

The crowds gather for the first passenger-carrying train to arrive at Bishops Waltham for twenty years. Railway enthusiast specials were uncommon at this time and numerous visitors were found mixing with local townsfolk to witness the event. Such was their enthusiasm that all vantage points were taken up. Bunting and Union Jacks make it a colourful scene.
PHILIP J. KELLEY

Having run round its train, Class 'C14' No. 30589 is prepared for the return journey to Botley. This was not the first visit of the class as No. 741 was tried on the branch between 17th July and 11th August 1907.
PHILIP J. KELLEY

The second of three special enthusiast workings on 2nd May 1953 when Class 'M7' 0—4—4T No. 30110 visited the line from Gosport on a tour of branch lines in the area. The train has set back into the yard to enable the engine to take water.
PHILIP J. KELLEY

Railway Correspondence and Travel Society organised a special passenger train from Eastleigh to Bishops Waltham. Formed of an ex-L & SW 'C14' class engine No. 30589 and two carriages of South Western origin, this train arrived at Botley from Eastleigh at 5.18 p.m. It was timed to leave for Bishops Waltham at 5.27 p.m. with a journey time over the branch of some sixteen minutes. Following a stopover at the terminus, the special set out on the return journey at 6.10 p.m. and a brief stop was made at the site of Durley Halt.

The following year saw another special passenger working on 3rd May, this time organised by the Stephenson Locomotive Society, when a rather more elaborate formation, consisting of a Class M7 0–4–4T No. 30110, sandwiched between four passenger vehicles, passed over the line. Two of the carriages were an ex-SECR push-pull set.

From 1954 Durley Crossing became unmanned and the gates were left unlocked, the normal position being across the road. Stop boards were provided 50 yards before the crossing in each direction and all trains had to stop and be hand signalled over the road by an accompanying porter who would be acting as train guard.

By the mid-1950s the great variety of traffic dealt with at Bishops Waltham had reduced sharply. Most of what was left was generated by Messrs. Dukes at the Abbey Mill. or coal and timber. Other occasional goods tended to be more localised than in previous years, the natural catchment area contracting in the face of direct road transport. The private sidings no longer yielded traffic, the brickworks had been disconnected by 1947, and Edwards Siding, unused for some years, had been taken out of use.

In the late 1950s ex LMS Ivatt Class '2MT' 2–6–2Ts began to work the solitary daily goods service. During this period it was policy to replace the ageing 'M7s' based at Eastleigh with the LMS type, so their appearance at Bishops Waltham could have been met with little surprise.

Perhaps sensing an uncertain future for the line, the Branch line Society paid a visit to the area on 7th March 1959, with yet another special train consisting of 'M7' No. 30111 borrowed from the Lymington branch and two passenger vehicles. This proved to be the last special train over the line.

The same year reflected the steady fall in traffic brought about by direct road deliveries when the daily service, already

April 1954 saw the retirement of Alice Tubbs who had been the crossing keeper at Durley since 1907. She is seen here with her brother Charlie, a lengthman in the local permanent way gang covering the branch, on the last day before the crossing became unmanned and operated by the engine crews. A relay bell was provided in the cottage up to this time to warn Alice of the departure of a train from Botley or Bishops Waltham, the codes being '4 pause 4' and '2 pause 2' respectively. While the crossing was manned, the gates were normally closed across the roadway.
SOUTHERN DAILY ECHO

Ex-LMS Ivatt 2—6—2T No. 41214 taking a break from shunting duties to take water on 1st March 1962. The brake van was allocated to the branch and marked 'To work between Botley and Bishops Waltham Only — Not in Common Use'. The vehicle was partitioned inside to provide accommodation for carrying parcels.   D. FEREDAY GLENN

The Ivatt tanks based at Eastleigh took over branch duties from the 'M7s' from about 1958, thus seeing out the final years of the Bishops Waltham line. This time No. 41293 has her tanks replenished before returning to Botley yard on 9th March 1962.
D. FEREDAY GLENN

A final glimpse of the station building with an Ivatt 2MT preparing the return goods service on 6th March 1962. By this time the service was reduced to twice weekly, in the face of the steadily falling demand.
JOHN BOSWORTH

curtailed to exclude Saturdays, in practice ran two to three times per week despite the daily provision in the working timetables. The inevitable end was clearly in sight and finally came on Friday 27th April 1962 with the passing of the last goods train.

Unlike passenger-carrying lines which often attracted a plethora of enthusiasts and locals, the last day passed without a ripple of attention. However, one enthusiast, Dr. Roy Coates, did present himself to record the event and recalled:

'Despite the fine warm weather of the preceding few days, the day was cold, very overcast and inclined to drizzle. At about 12.10 p.m.

Station and crossing c.1961. The Southern Railway enamel station name survived until closure.   LENS OF SUTTON

the train reversed into the down bay, propelled by Ivatt Class 2MT N. 41328. The driver collected the token from the signal box, and we set off down the branch with 41328 running bunker first. The site of Durley Halt was shown us, and two dogs from a nearby farm gave their regular 50-yard chase along the track. At Bishops Waltham shunting took place, while the best use was made of the poor photographic weather. The remarshalled train was left standing in the loop while the crew visited the station, emerging laden with detonators. We departed at 1 p.m. with a fusilade of detonators from both ends of the train. Instead of slowing to 5 m.p.h. and hooting vigorously at occupation crossings we came to a dead stop, and proceeded again to the accompaniment of more detonations.'

The dust now settled, the contractors moved in to remove the permanent way and other redundant material. A hopeful flicker of renaissance occurred just prior to this, however, when the Hampshire Narrow Gauge Society became interested in purchasing the trackbed to lay a 2 ft. gauge line from a point outside Botley (actually Maddoxford) to just south of the level crossing at Bishops Waltham where a new station was proposed. These plans lingered on until around 1964, but nothing positive was undertaken and the idea simply faded into oblivion.

The obliteration of the Bishops Waltham station site in the late 1960s to make way for road improvements was predictable enough, but surely the ruthless act of demolishing that unique station building was nothing short of civic vandalism.

The A333 road to Winchester, looking towards Newtown after closure. Following the abolition of signalling, the crossing gates were manually operated in accordance with Rules 99-107, with the main gates closed across the railway. These had to be closed and locked across the road three minutes before a down train was due to arrive and immediately before an up train was due to leave.

JOHN BOSWORTH

The brickworks, viewed from the Winchester Road c.1900. On the left is Claylands House, formerly the residence of Mark Blanchard.
COURTESY JOHN BOSWORTH

Taken from the west, looking back towards the town, this view shows the various bricks and other terracotta stacked to the right of one of the 'beehive' kilns. A small tramway system was used to transport materials around the site. The private siding was usually worked twice a week with the engine propelling between 6-10 wagons at a time. Outward traffic consisted of bricks, tiles, terracotta pipes, blue bricks etc. Coal was brought in to fuel the kilns. When the engine was ready to leave the station yard, the train would be taken into the back siding serving Messrs. Smith and a whistle would be sounded to warn for the gates over Sawmill Lane to be opened. At the works a raised platform was provided at the end of the siding to aid loading. Most traffic was dealt with by hand but it is believed a crane was provided at one time.
AUTHORS' COLLECTION

An early 20th-century view of a group of workmen in front of one of the 'beehive' kilns. The products from the Newtown works were used in several famous buildings including Buckingham Palace and the Victoria and Albert Museum. In 1888 the LSWR ordered 1.5 million bricks from Blanchards for a substantial part of their estimated annual requirement.
COURTESY JOHN BOSWORTH

APPENDIX 1
BLANCHARD & THE CLAY COMPANY

There is little doubt that the formation of the Bishops Waltham Clay Company by Sir Arthur Helps was a major factor in bringing the railway to the town. The two are inextricably linked, sharing many of the same directors in the early years of both companies. Indeed, some of the BW Railway business was transacted at meetings on the premises of the Clay Company.

Events began in 1860 when Mr. Helps undertook test borings on the site of the clay deposits located to the north-west of the town. These lay at the intersection of the 'Reading Beds' and 'London Clay'and were previously described as having 'some of the finest clay beds in the United Kingdom'. Helps' samples were analysed by Coades Terra-Cotta manufacturers at their Lambeth premises and reported on favourably. As a consequence, Helps purchased the Vernon Hill Estate on which the clay beds were situated, and he began to develop the new workings.

The Bishops Waltham Clay Company was formed in September 1862. The authorised capital of just over £80,000 was applied in the construction of the works themselves and the provision of cottages for the employees in Victoria Road and Albert Road.

The first products manufactured by the new company were 'Black' bricks and tiles, some of the bricks being used in the construction of Blackfriars Bridge over the Thames. From February 1866 some fine art pottery was produced on an experimental basis, some of the craftsmen involved coming from established firms in Staffordshire. However this venture was only destined to last just under two years.

The Clay Company suffered financial failure in 1866 and in April 1867 went into liquidation with serious effect on the already financially insecure Bishops Waltham Railway Company.

Production was continued until December of that year and, following a period of disuse, the works were taken over by Mark Henry Blanchard. Activities were got under way again, steadily increasing until in 1880 Blanchard sold his established London business at Lambeth and concentrated manufacture at what became known as the Newtown Works.

The reputation of Blanchard's products became second to none and Bishops Waltham became the foremost brick works in Hampshire. Manufactured goods at this time included ridge, hip, valley and angle tiles, and red and blue bricks. The terra-cotta was considered superior to most, owing to skilful mixing and firing which resulted in valued qualities of hardness, texture, colour and finish. Products from Newtown were used far and wide, finding their way to buildings in America, Egypt, South Africa, South America, Holland and Poland. Closer to home, buildings containing Blanchard's terra-cotta included Buckingham Palace, Victoria and Albert Museum, Cannon Street station, Charing Cross Hotel and, more locally, the Prudential Building and Post Office in Southampton. The impressive Shawford Viaduct on the extension of the Didcot, Newbury & Southampton Railway opened in 1891 used many locally produced bricks, many of which were supplied from Newtown.

The area of the works extended to some 20 acres and included workshops, engine houses, drying houses, a stable for eight horses, pug mills, weighbridge, a gas house and a 'Hoffmans' annular kiln. Apart from the siding from the branch, which was provided with a loop, around the 1870s the complex included around 970 yards of narrow gauge tramway. This was later cut back according to the clay workings prevailing at the time. Small 'tipper' type wagons were used on the tramway to move clay from the workings to the storage tip where they would be pulled up an inclined ramp by a stationary gas engine remembered as running all day when production was in full swing.

In February 1892 Mark Blanchard died and his business was taken over by his son, also Mark Henry. Around this time over 200 men were employed in the works and it is recalled that they worked to a bell rung in the yard. This could apparently be heard all over Bishops Waltham.

Mark Henry Blanchard Snr. in 1891. This was a publicity photograph following a demonstration of the company's fireproof terracotta staircase. In the background the private siding can be seen curving away back towards the station.
COURTESY JOHN BOSWORTH

At the time of the First World War the firm became a limited company and later in 1918 was taken over by Messrs. Elliotts of Millbank Wharf, Northam. Under this new ownership the plant was modernised and beehive type kilns and an eighteen chamber continuous burning kiln were installed. Production of good quality building materials continued but with modern equipment, the number of employees had more than halved.

Fire damage in the 1930s and the effects of a bomb landing by the Works in the Second War did not disrupt production although manufacture was in steady decline. The War did stop production in 1941, although this was resumed in 1946 when the demand for brick products to repair bomb damaged buildings grew. By this time the siding from the station had been truncated and the connection taken out, presumably the firm were using road transport for their products. The siding was abolished officially in December 1947.

It would appear that by 1953 demand had cut back severely as Messrs. Elliotts proposed to auction Blanchard's Brick and Tile-Works (it was still known by this name) on 18th June. The sale catalogue listed the works, all buildings and land amounting to 43 acres. Interestingly, the average annual production figures for the period 1949 to 1952 were given as:

Bricks	1,450,900	Tiles & Fittings	654,500
Agricultural Pipes	64,800	Briquettes	83,000

For reasons not recorded the sale was withdrawn and Messrs. Elliotts continued production until 1956 when the Works finally closed.

An excellent aerial view of the town and station area taken from the east. At the top of the picture the brickworks can clearly be seen nestling in front of the large chalk workings. From left to right the station building, water tank and goods shed can be discerned, with the formation leading north towards the gas works.

AEROFILMS

APPENDIX 2
BISHOPS WALTHAM GAS & COKE COMPANY

The Bishops Waltham Gas and Coke Company held their first meeting at the Crown Hotel on the 14th April 1863. The directors unanimously elected Mr. Bettesworth Pitt Shearer as Chairman. (He was also chairman of the BW Railway Co.) Discussion took place as to the site for the works and following the consideration of three alternatives, the company eventually settled for a 200-year leasing of land from Arthur Helps at a nominal rent of £5 p.a. The ¼ acre site was part of the clay workings to the north of the station described as a 'Chalk Dell' and could benefit from the use of the Clay Company's siding. A road access was also made from Lower Lane.

Mr. George Garnett, gas engineer from Ryde, was asked to prepare a specification for the erection of the works, and a Frome company, Messrs. Cockey & Sons' tender for £900 was accepted on 12th October. Messrs. Rilson & Ridley, who were completing the construction of Bishops Waltham station, were engaged to clear the site for £25 in December 1863.

In February 1864 it was reported that:

'The Works are now nearly completed and will shortly be able to supply Gas. The mains laying is completed and the pipes are laid on for several consumers including the Railway Company.'

Garnett, in a letter to the directors, elaborated further:

'The buildings are all erected and the Gasholder Tank is nearly complete. The Retort Benches are complete and the Retorts set. A Condenser is erected and the Scrubber and Purifiers are nearly complete.'

The works were opened and production began in March 1864. The price of gas to consumers was set at 7/6d per 1,000 cubic feet, with a set charge of £3 p.a. for each public street lamp, 'being lighted from dusk till 12 p.m. except five nights each moon and extinguished during the three summer months, an exception being the lamp in the square, which is lit all night. This charge to be £4 p.a.'

The town of Bishops Waltham was thus believed to have been lighted for the first time on 4th March 1864, making it one of the earliest towns in Hampshire to be provided with gas street lighting. Until August 1879 the lighting, extinguishing and cleaning of public lamps was undertaken by Henry Collis, an employee of the Gas Company. However, from this date the responsibility was contracted out to an agent, the first being Frank Davis who performed the task for £16 p.a. Eventually the duty fell to the Corporation Lighting Inspectors from September 1882 when lamps were then metered at 5/- per 1,000 cubic feet.

Increasing demand for gas during the 1865 to 1880 period led to pressure to improve and increase the plant. A new iron retort and two clay retorts were installed in 1865 at an estimated cost of £28. Repairs and replacements to retorts and other plant took place during the 1870s until a major upgrading of the works in the late 1890s when three new clay retorts (estimated cost £100) and a new washer and purifier installed. A second gas holder to hold 6,000 cubic feet was also constructed by Messrs. Cockey & Son for £396. Other extensive but unspecified repairs were undertaken at the same time at a cost of £113 17s 3d. The new gas holder was brought into use in February 1901 along with the commissioning of a new enlarged mains system from the works and new meters and governors. A coal storage shed was also erected.

As with numerous other gas companies at the time, the Bishops Waltham works were highly profitable up to the early 1890s. Relatively low production costs, a high output and demand sufficient to set a price for gas which resulted in high profit and an excellent annual return for the shareholders. Dividends paid out amounted to between £4 to £6 per cent. upon paid up capital. The success of the company can be measured by the fact that the charge to private consumers was reduced from 7/6d per 1,000 cubic feet to 6/8d from 25th March 1877 and to 5/10d with effect from 25th March 1879. The pressure from the LSWR previously mentioned resulted in a further reduction to 5/- from 25th March 1880. A reduction in the annual charge for street lamps was also made in January 1877 from £3 to £2-10s per lamp.

The gas works, located at the far end of the line. The gasometer seen here was a 'double lift' type erected when production of gas on the site ceased in 1932. Prior to this the siding was in daily use transporting large quantities of small fire coal for the retorts. Complete trains of coal were not unknown as usually three out of the four retorts would be in operation. The retorts were emptied about 3.45 p.m. each day and the consequent coke removed and doused with water. This would provide the primary outgoing material although tar and creosote were also produced. Most of the coke was sold to the local coal merchants but some went down the branch destined further afield. To aid the handling of coal, a narrow gauge system raised on trestles ran alongside part of the siding and into the retort house in a semi-circle. Small tipper wagons were pushed by hand along the system which contained no points or loop. AEROFILMS

However, the lucrative position enjoyed by the company was to change with the miners' strike of 1894. The resulting large increase in coal prices at the pits had a considerable impact on production costs and in subsequent years shareholders were dismayed to learn that the directors could no longer recommend a return on their investment. Furthermore expanding demand around the turn of the century required much extra capital. The days of an easy return for little effort were over.

Various collieries supplied coal to the gas works over the years, resulting in a wide range of private owner wagons over the branch. As mentioned on page 29, from the opening both Brays Down Coal Co. and the Somersetshire Coal Co. were the main suppliers. From 1877 the records show payments to the Radstock Coal & Wagon Co., Messrs. Stephenson, Clarke & Co. from around 1898 and in the early years of this century Renwick, Wilton & Co., the Midland Coal & Canal Co. and the Colliery Supply Co.

From January 1898 the Gas Company appointed a Mr. Churcher to cart coals from the station to the works for 10d. per ton including trimming. Early in 1900 Messrs. Blanchard & Co. took over this role for the same terms. In May 1923 this contract was awarded to the Colliery Supply Co. at the rate of 2/6d per ton.

Commencing in July 1930, negotiations with the Gosport and District Gas Company resulted in the Bishops Waltham Works being taken over, the official agreement to this effect being sealed in March 1931. The transfer of all plant and equipment was effected on 1st January 1932 when, after an independent existence of just under 68 years, the Bishops Waltham Gas & Coke Company was wound up.

APPENDIX 3

BISHOPS WALTHAM RAILWAY
DIRECTORS AND SHAREHOLDING 1862

	No. of Shares	
Bettesworth Pitt Shearer	500	Chairman 7/1862 to 3/1863
William Henry Stone MP	1000	Chairman 3/1863 to 2/1869
Arthur Helps	1000	
George Clark	200	
Edward Wyatt	100	
Edward Woodville Ricketts	1000	Resigned 5/1864
Theodore Martin	2000	
John Alldin Moore	1000	
Charles Gummer	400	
Frances Clark	50	
Frederick Savage	10	
Charles Privett	10	
William Killick	10	

BISHOPS WALTHAM RAILWAY DIRECTORS 1881

Samuel Coates Ridley	Chairman
William Gold Buchanan	
William Hendry Vause	
Clement Stackhouse Helps	
Rev. Sidney Porter	

APPENDIX 4

BISHOPS WALTHAM RAILWAY
PREFERENTIAL SHAREHOLDERS 1862

Augusta Murray	5
Catherine E. Nixon	10
William Glover	33
Anthony Ward Ritson	129
Samuel Coates Ridley	
William Henry Stone MP	37
Theodore Martin	8
William Glover (plumber)	22
Imperial Mercantile Credit	65
William McKewan	64
Charles Cousins	64
John Sherry	15
Thomas Geo. Williams	10
Samuel Clayton	10
Edward Dearle	5
Frederick William Wyatt	14
William Twick	10
Edward Smith	14

APPENDIX 5

LOCOMOTIVES KNOWN TO HAVE WORKED
THE BRANCH

Steam Railmotors Nos. 1*, 2, 9* 10* 8	No. 1 Nov. 1904
1-10 all run in at some stage	1905-1914
'A1' 0–6–0T No. 734	1907
'C14' 2–2–0T Nos. 742, 741	c.1907
'C14' 0–4–0T Nos. 101, 147	
'O2' 0–4–4T No. 217	1911
'D1' 0–4–2T Nos. 240, 260*, 616*	1930s
'M7' 0–4–4T No. 376, 30033, 30375, 30480	
'O2' 0–4–4T Nos. 206, 211, 236*	1920s/1930s
Ivatt Class 2 2–6–2T No. 41328*	1960s
Standard Class 4 2–6–0 No. 76059*	1960s
'T1' 0–4–4T No. 9	c.1915-1920
'M7' 0–4–4T No. 24	c.1918
Nos. 22, 23, 26, 27, 28, 29	c.1915-1920
RCTS Special 'C14' 0–4–0T No. 30489*	

* Photos of engines held.

APPENDIX 6

BISHOPS WALTHAM RAILWAY
HALF YEARLY TRAFFIC RETURNS 1863 to 1867

To 12/1863		To 6/1864	
Passenger	£334 1 6	Passenger	£308 12 10
Goods	£231 6 7	Goods	£261 13 6
Total	£565 8 1	Total	£570 6 4
45% Working Expenses	£254 8 8	45% Working Expenses	£256 12 10
Profit	£310 19 5	Profit	£313 13 6

To 12/1864		To 6/1865	
Passenger	£407 15 3	Passenger	£308 16 5
Goods	£278 18 8	Goods	£210 3 0
Total	£686 13 11	Total	£518 19 5
45% Working Expenses	£309 0 3	45% Working Expenses	£233 10 9
Profit	£377 13 8	Profit	£285 8 8

To 12/1865		To 6/1866	
Passenger	£401 9 6	Passenger	£295 7 11
Goods	£204 4 9	Goods	£246 18 5
Total	£605 14 3	Total	£542 6 4
45% Working Expenses	£272 11 5	45% Working Expenses	£244 0 10
Profit	£333 2 10	Profit	£298 5 6

To 12/1866		To 6/1867	
Passenger	£317 15 11	Passenger	£251 11 4
Goods	£208 2 11	Goods	£189 13 4
Total	£525 18 10	Total	£441 4 8
45% Working Expenses	£236 13 5	45% Working Expenses	£198 11 1
Profit	£289 5 5	Profit	£242 13 7

To 12/1867	
Passenger	£282 12 1
Goods	£177 5 9
Total	£459 17 10
45% Working Expenses	£206 19 0
Profit	£252 18 10

APPENDIX 7

Year	BISHOPS WALTHAM Station Master	Carrier	BOTLEY Station Master	Carrier
1867	–	–	James Whitney	Bastable
1871	–	–	James Whitney	Bastable
1875	James Whitney	Lomer, Emmett	James Whitney	Bastable
1880	James Whitney	Henry Lomer, Peter Emmett	James Whitney	Bastable
1889	James Whitney	Lomer, Emmett	James Whitney	James Court
1895	James Whitney	Lomer, Emmett	James Whitney	Court
1899	Albert Kneller		Albert Kneller	
1907	Charles William Colbourne	Paskins	Edward W. Croome	Court
1911	Charles William Colbourne	Arthur Paskins, Hibberd	Edward W. Croome	Herbert Court
1915	Charles William Colbourne	Paskins, Arnett, Hibberd	Harry W. Hayter	Court
1920	Sidney James Everny	Paskins, Hibberd	Herbert Wright Jones	Hargreaves
1924	Blount		Jones	
1927	Charles Henry Blount	Paskins	Herbert Wright Jones	Hargreaves
1931	Not known	Paskins	Herbert Wright Jones	Hargreaves
1935	–	Paskins	Not known	Not known
1939	–	Paskins	Not known	Paskins, Cox
1942	Supervised from Botley		Bill Smith	
1952	Supervised from Botley		Frank Holland	
1956	Supervised from Botley		Harry Newman	
1961	Supervised from Botley		Vic Simms	

BISHOPS WALTHAM STAFFING c.1919

Station Master	Charles Colbourne
1 Booking Clerk	Mr. Woods
1 Goods Clerk	Zeb. Andrews
1 Signalman	Tom Cuell
2 Porter/Signalmen	Steve Goulding and Percy Honour
1 Porter	George Elford
1 Passenger Guard	George Padwick
Engine Shed	
2 Drivers	Bert Bath and Frank Wills
2 Firemen	George Smith and Jack Gamblin
1 Engine Cleaner	? Arthur Green or 'Punch' King

S.R. STAFF CENSUS 1926

Bishops Waltham	Botley
1 Booking Clerk, Class 5	1 Booking Clerk, Class 5
2 Drivers	4 Gangers
2 Firemen	1 Sub-Ganger
1 Cleaner	12 Undermen
1 Station Master, Class 5	1 Station Master, Class 3
2 Porters, Class 1	4 Porters
2 Porter/Signalmen, Class 5	2 Signalmen
	1 Crossing Keeper (Durley)
	1 Checker

BOTLEY STAFFING c.1955

Station Master	Harry Newman
2 Signalmen	Bill Carpenter and Gerry Watts
1 Porter/Signalman	Mears
2 Porters	Doug Dowdy, Arthur 'Togo' Gibson
1 Goods Checker	Bill Hillier
2 Junior Clerks	Norman Beckett and David Luckett

APPENDIX 8

WORKING TIMETABLE — 1883 (Weekdays)

DOWN TRAINS	a.m.	a.m.	a.m.	a.m.	p.m.	p.m.	p.m.
Botley	8.45	9.25	10.03	11.28	1.55	5.45	8.12
Bishops Waltham	8.57	9.37	10.15	11.40	2.07	5.57	8.24

UP TRAINS	a.m.	a.m.	a.m.	a.m.	p.m.	p.m.	p.m.
Bishops Waltham	8.15	9.00	9.50	11.05	12.55	4.35	7.00
Botley	8.26	9.12	9.59	11.12	1.07	4.47	7.12

WORKING TIMETABLE — 1905 (Weekdays)

DOWN TRAINS	a.m.	a.m.	a.m.	a.m.	a.m.	p.m.	p.m.	p.m. Goods	p.m.	p.m.	p.m.	p.m.	p.m.	p.m.
Botley	7.50	8.42	9.25	10.15	11.05	12.15	1.45	2.00	3.06	3.55	5.57	7.30	8.00	8.55
Bishops Waltham	8.05	8.54	9.37	10.27	11.20	12.27	1.57	2.10	3.18	4.07	6.09	7.40	8.10	9.07

UP TRAINS	a.m.	a.m.	a.m. Light engine	a.m.	a.m.		p.m.	p.m.	p.m.	p.m.	p.m. Goods	p.m.	p.m.	p.m.
Bishops Waltham	8.20	9.00	9.15	9.47	10.38	11.50	1.15	2.45	3.35	4.45	4.58	7.10	7.45	8.30
Botley	8.30	9.12	9.23	9.59	10.50	12.02	1.25	2.57	3.47	4.57	5.13	7.20	7.55	8.42

WORKING TIMETABLE — 1919 (Weekdays)

DOWN TRAINS	a.m.	a.m.	a.m. Goods	p.m.	p.m.	p.m. Light engine	p.m.	p.m.	p.m.
Botley	8.27	9.20	11.10	12.15	2.10	3.30	4.10	5.15	7.05
Durley	8.31	9.24		12.19	2.14		4.14	5.19	7.09
Bishops Waltham	8.37	9.30	11.22	12.25	2.20	3.38	4.20	5.25	7.15

UP TRAINS	a.m.	a.m.	a.m.	a.m.	p.m.	p.m.	p.m.	p.m.	p.m.
Bishops Waltham	7.55	8.45	10.15	11.40	1.40	3.00	3.45	4.35	6.30
Durley	8.01	8.51	10.21	11.46	1.46		3.51	4.41	6.36
Botley	8.05	8.55	10.25	11.50	1.50	3.12	3.55	4.45	6.40

WORKING TIMETABLE — 1933 (Weekdays)

DOWN TRAINS	a.m.	p.m.
Botley	8.50	3.45
Bishops Waltham	9.07	4.00

UP TRAINS	a.m.	p.m.
Bishops Waltham	9.35	5.25
Botley	9.50	5.42

WORKING TIMETABLE — 1939, 1942 and 1960/61 (Weekdays)

DOWN TRAINS	1939 a.m.	1942 a.m.	1960/61 a.m. SX
Botley	8.55	9.30	10.00
Bishops Waltham	9.10	9.45	10.20

UP TRAINS	1939 a.m.	1942 a.m.	1960/61 a.m. SX
Bishops Waltham	10.30	11.30	11.10
Botley	10.47	11.47	11.30

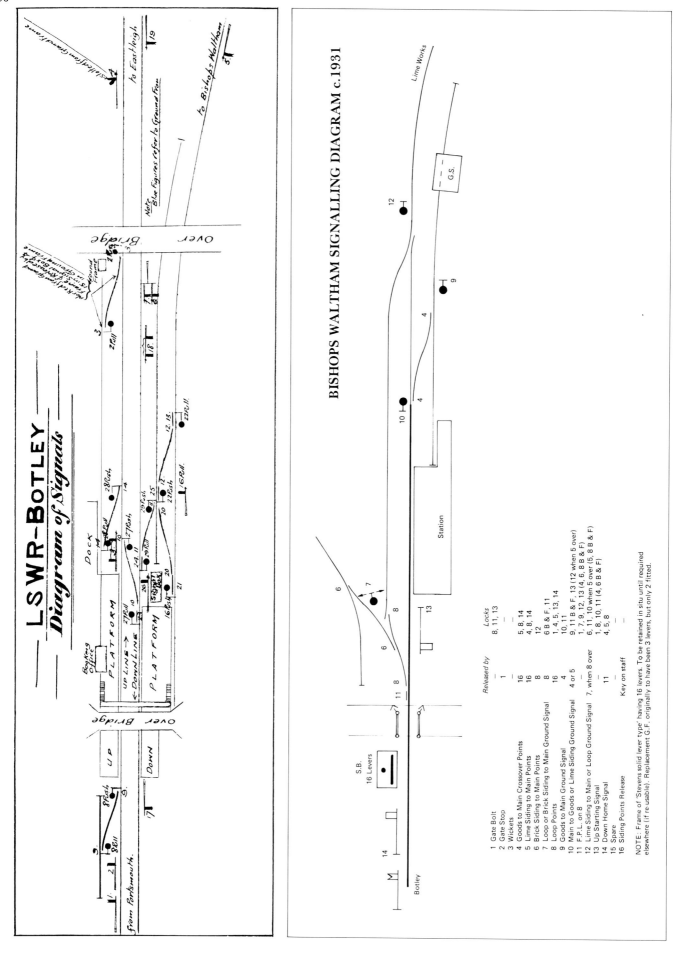

LSWR-Botley

Diagram of Signals

BISHOPS WALTHAM SIGNALLING DIAGRAM c.1931

	Released by	Locks
1 Gate Bolt	—	8, 11, 13
2 Gate Stop	1	—
3 Wickets	—	—
4 Goods to Main Crossover Points	16	5, 8, 14
5 Lime Siding to Main Points	16	4, 8, 14
6 Brick Siding to Main Points	8	12
7 Loop or Brick Siding to Main Ground Signal	8	6 B & F, 11
8 Loop Points	16	1, 4, 5, 13, 14
9 Goods to Main Ground Signal	4	10, 11
10 Main to Goods or Lime Siding Ground Signal	4 or 5	9, 11 B & F, 13 (12 when 5 over)
11 F.P.L. on 8	—	1, 7, 9, 12, 13 (4, 6, 8 B & F)
12 Lime Siding to Main or Loop Ground Signal	7, when 8 over	6, 11, 10 when 5 over (5, 8 B & F)
13 Up Starting Signal	—	1, 8, 10, 11 (4, 6 B & F)
14 Down Home Signal	11	4, 5, 8
15 Spare	—	—
16 Siding Points Release	Key on staff	—

S.B.
16 Levers

Botley

NOTE: Frame of 'Stevens solid lever type' having 16 levers. To be retained in situ until required elsewhere (if re-usable). Replacement G.F. originally to have been 3 levers, but only 2 fitted.

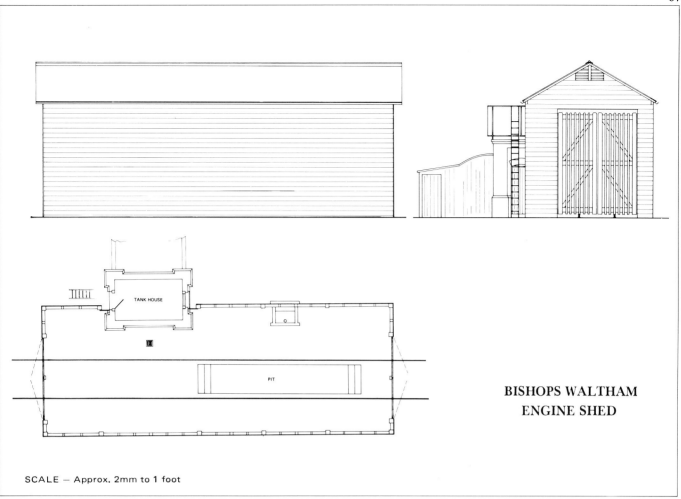

**BISHOPS WALTHAM
ENGINE SHED**

SCALE — Approx. 2mm to 1 foot

BISHOPS WALTHAM WATER TOWER

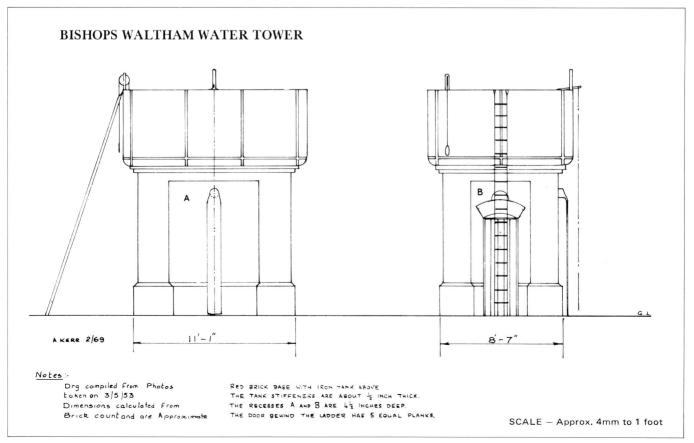

A KERR 2/69

11'-1"

8'-7"

Notes :-
Drg compiled from Photos
taken on 3/5/53
Dimensions calculated from
Brick count and are Approximate

RED BRICK BASE WITH IRON TANK ABOVE
THE TANK STIFFENERS ARE ABOUT ½ INCH THICK.
THE RECESSES A AND B ARE 4½ INCHES DEEP.
THE DOOR BEHIND THE LADDER HAS 5 EQUAL PLANKS.

SCALE — Approx. 4mm to 1 foot

BOTLEY STATION BUILDING

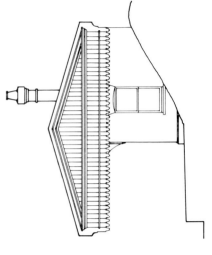

PLATFORM ELEVATION

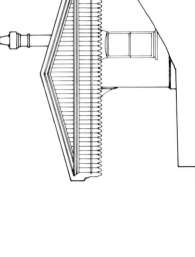

END ELEVATION

SCALE — Approx. 2mm to 1 foot

BOTLEY STATION BUILDING

FORECOURT ELEVATION

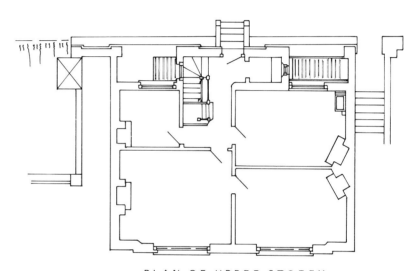

PLAN OF UPPER STOREY

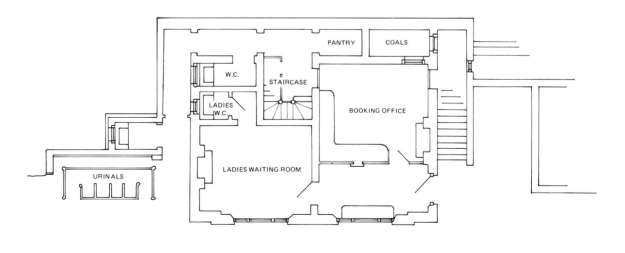

PANTRY

COALS

W.C.

STAIRCASE

LADIES
W.C.

BOOKING OFFICE

URINALS

LADIES WAITING ROOM

PLAN OF GROUND FLOOR

SCALE — Approx. 2mm to 1 foot

BOTLEY STATION FOOTBRIDGE

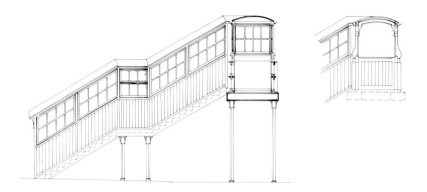

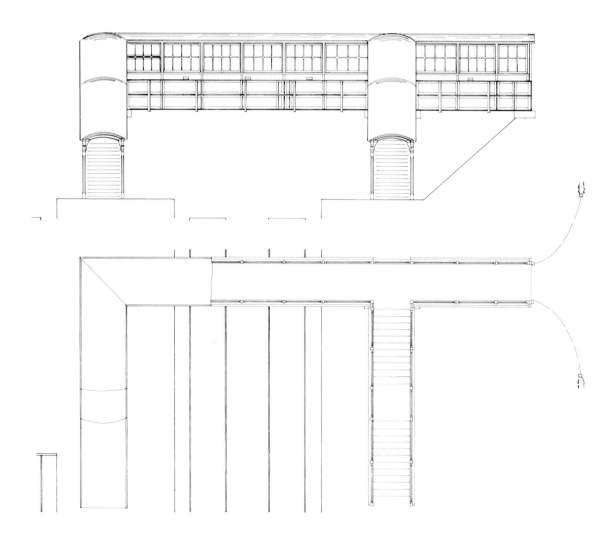

SCALE — Approx. 2mm to 1 foot

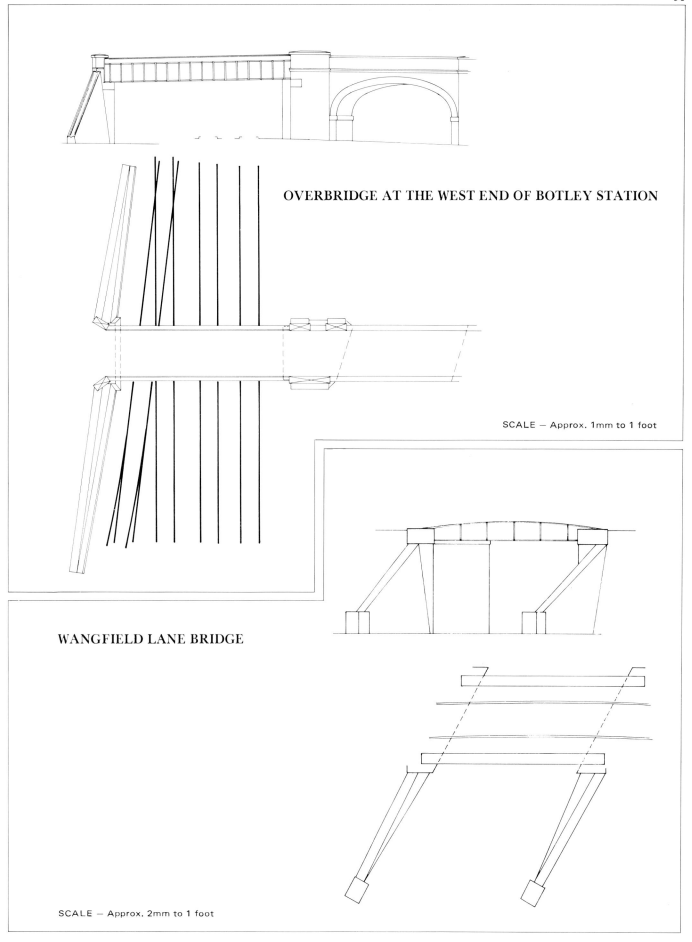

OVERBRIDGE AT THE WEST END OF BOTLEY STATION

SCALE — Approx. 1mm to 1 foot

WANGFIELD LANE BRIDGE

SCALE — Approx. 2mm to 1 foot

ACKNOWLEDGEMENTS

This book is the culmination of many, many hours of painstaking research, but at the same time it has been a delight to compile, enriched by the warm reception my co-author and I have received from former staff and local people who have been so willing to share their intimate recollections of a time when the trains ran up to 'Waltham and the station was the focal point of the town and centre for the industries of the lower Meon Valley.

First and foremost we must acknowledge John King who really got us started on the venture and has given active encouragement throughout and many leads. Thanks are also due to John Bosworth, who kindly gave us free access to his extensive photographic collection of the Bishops Waltham area and guidance on historical matters concerning the town; Harry Newman, a former Botley station master, whose vivid memories and enthusiasm gently coaxed us along and who sadly died before seeing this account published (a special thanks to Peg for the generous refreshment); Archie Blaver, Charlie Pitman and Tom Saunders, whose recollections of the branch provided an insight into the line in the early years of the century; Jim King, whose first-hand knowledge of the coal and carrier businesses operating from Bishops Waltham bridged many information gaps and enlightened us regarding events during the period of the Second World War; Catherine Tickner for allowing us to reproduce her late husband's photographs; and finally in this section Reg Randall who never fails to turn up an 'ace' or two.

Our warmest appreciation is also extended to the following individuals and organisations: Don Bradley for information on locomotive allocations; Michael Clode; Reg Cockle; Dennis Cullum; H. P. Edwards; John Fairman for helpful advice and gently corrective influence; Bert Gibson; Graham Hawkins; Simon Matthews for several leads; Alack Osman; Mrs. D. Robertson; Dennis Tilman and fellow colleagues in the South Western Circle; J. E. Smith [Messrs. J. E. Smith (Portsmouth) Ltd.]; Vic Wakefield; Roy Zachar; Botley & Curdridge Local History Society; Messrs. James Duke & Son Ltd., in particular Tom Duke and Paul Cordery, who not only gave their time but also permitted free access to the company records; Hampshire County Library, in particular Phillipa Stevens who always retains a smile despite the most oblique enquiry; Hampshire Museum Service, especially Jan Grant for all the chasing-up; Hampshire Record Office; Portsmouth City Library; Public Record Office, Kew; Southampton City Libary; The South Western Circle; Winchester City Museum, in particular Karen Parker. The following newspapers were also consulted: *Hampshire Chronicle; Hampshire Observer; Southampton Times; Hampshire Independant; Southern Daily Echo; Hampshire Telegraph; The News, Portsmouth.*

Thanks must also be recorded to the following for photographic contributions: Aerofilms Ltd., A. E. Bennett, Sean Bolan, A. W. Burgess, W. A. Camwell, H. C. Casserley, R. M. Casserley, John J. Davis, Les Elsey, D. Fereday Glenn, Philip Kelley, Lens of Sutton, Rev. David Littlefair, Malcolm Snellgrove and the late Jack Tickner.

Our grateful thanks to June Judge for patiently coping with a handwritten manuscript and Paul Karau for his usual mastery at the helm, tempering our exuberance. We, in deference, can only express our humble gratitude.   *Roger Simmonds*

BIBLIOGRAPHY

The following books and periodicals have been consulted:

The London & South Western Railway, Volumes 1 & 2 by R. A. Williams. Published by David & Charles.
A History of Botley Station by Violet Cooke. Published by Botley & Curdridge Local History Society.
Bishops Waltham in Old Postcards by John Bosworth. Published by the European Library.
Newtown & Clay 1860-1957 by Ted Pitman.
A Gazetteer of Brick & Tile Works in Hampshire. Published by Hampshire Industrial Archaeological Group.
Mates Guide to Hampshire Towns & Villages. Published 1906.
Various issues of the LSWR and SR Magazines.
Various issues of the *Railway Magazine.*
The Railway Observer. RCTS.
Strawberries and the LSWR by F. C. Neill. South Western Circular.